BEHOLD YOUR MOTHER

Mary, the Cross,
and the
Power of Reparation

A Mission of Consolation,

Intimacy and Devotion

Allan Smith

Published by: Bishop Sheen Today
www.bishopsheentoday.com

Title: Behold Your Mother. Mary, the Cross, and the Power of Reparation. A Mission of Consolation, Intimacy, and Devotion.

Compiled by Allan J. Smith. Includes bibliographical references.

Book formatting and design by Ajayi Isaac
mailto:smeplegacy@gmail.com/ +2348162435897

Identifiers:

Paperback: 978-1-997627-61-6

eBook: 978-1-997627-62-3
Hardcover: 978-1-997627-63-0

Subjects: Jesus Christ — The Blessed Virgin Mary — Prayer
and Meditation – The Holy Face Devotion - St. Thérèse of
Lisieux – Archbishop Fulton J. Sheen – Lives of the Saints

BEHOLD YOUR MOTHER

Mary, the Cross, and the Power of Reparation.
A Mission of Consolation, Intimacy, and Devotion.
A Sheen Mission Series - Volume II

The Sheen Mission Series invites you to walk with Archbishop Fulton J. Sheen in prayer, reparation, and renewal — a journey of the Holy Face, the Cross, the Eucharist and Our Blessed Mother.

Description:

Behold Your Mother is the second volume in the Sheen Mission Series — a Marian companion for those who wish to walk more closely with Our Lady at the foot of the Cross.

Here you will discover meditations on the Seven Sorrows of Mary, reflections on her role in salvation history, and the consoling strength she offers to those who suffer. With Archbishop Fulton Sheen as a guide, this volume invites you to enter into Mary's tender care and to experience her love as Mother and Queen.

Series Note:

This book is the second of four volumes in *The Sheen Mission Series*, a collection of spiritual companions for personal devotion and parish renewal:

"When Jesus said to John, 'Behold your mother,' He gave us His Mother to be ours. No one can ever say that he is alone in the world when he has Mary as his Mother."

— Archbishop Fulton J. Sheen

Dedication:

**To Our Lady
of the Holy Name of God
who leads us to her son**

&

**To all souls
who stand faithfully
at the foot of the Cross
and take to heart,
the words of Christ**

"Behold Your Mother"

J M J

Archbishop Fulton J. Sheen's episcopal motto was *Da Per Matrem Me Venire* — "Grant that I may come to You through Your Mother." Following this wisdom, Sheen often urged the faithful to draw closer to Christ through Mary, echoing the counsel of St. Louis de Montfort: *"To Jesus through Mary."*

This book continues Sheen's mission by presenting his Marian insights alongside the spirituality of St. Thérèse of the Child Jesus and the Holy Face. Together, their words offer a treasury of wisdom, devotion, and encouragement for the journey of faith.

The aim of this devotional mission is threefold: to encourage the virtue of daily prayer, to deepen love for Our Blessed Mother, and to foster a more intimate union with Jesus through her. Within these pages, readers will also discover many traditional Catholic prayers to aid them in their spiritual life.

It is my prayer that these reflections will find their way into homes, hospital rooms, retreat centers, and chapels — wherever souls search for hope and meaning. In opening these pages, may they discover anew that Christ and His Mother are near, leading them always to mercy and peace.

Archbishop Sheen once wrote that *"books are the most patient of teachers."* May this book be a companion for you, offering encouragement and practical wisdom as you draw ever closer to Jesus through Mary.

Sit Nomen Domini Benedictum!

Blessed be the Name of the Lord!

Allan J. Smith
September 8, 2025

Feast of the Nativity of the Blessed Virgin Mary

Table of Contents

XXV

Foreword

"To a great extent, the level of any civilization is the level of its womanhood."

— Archbishop Fulton J. Sheen

In every age, the Blessed Virgin Mary has stood as the model of purity, love, and sacrifice. And in our time — a time of wounded hearts and weary souls — she shines all the more brightly. This book is a call to return to her embrace, to listen anew to her sorrows, and to join her in the work of reparation.

When Archbishop Fulton J. Sheen spoke of the Blessed Virgin Mary, he did not speak merely of doctrine or sentiment. He spoke of a *Person*. He loved her with the fire of a son and the reverence of a priest. He once said, "She is the one whom every man loves when he loves a woman,". For Sheen, Mary was not only the Mother of God — she was the Mother of us all. At the foot of the Cross, mysteriously, she became our co-sufferer, our co-redeemer, and the spiritual Mother of every soul who longs for Heaven.

This book — the second volume in this mission series — is born from the pulpit, the confessional, and the quiet tears of countless souls who have knelt before the image of the Sorrowful Mother. It is a pilgrimage in print: a retreat with Mary at the foot of the Cross.

These meditations draw from parish missions, Marian devotions, and the theology of saints like St. Louis de Montfort, St. Alphonsus Liguori, and St. Therese of the Child Jesus. But above all, they echo the voice of Sheen — who taught us that Calvary is not just a place to witness, but a place to join.

Let Mary take your hand. Let her lead you back to the Heart of her Son. And as she whispers in your soul: *"Behold, your mother"* — may you echo back, *"Behold, my love."*

Introduction:
Why Mary? Why Now?

At the heart of every true renewal in the Church, there is always a woman. Not just any woman — but *the* Woman. The one clothed with the sun. The one whose "yes" changed the course of human history. The one who stood at the foot of the Cross and silently offered her Son back to the Father for the salvation of souls.

Today, the world is aching. Families are broken. Confusion reigns. And the Church — bruised but beloved — stands again at Calvary. Now more than ever, we must behold our Mother.

This is not a poetic suggestion. It is a divine command. *"Behold your mother,"* Jesus said from the Cross — not just to John, but to you, to me, to the Church across time. And in that moment, Mary's motherhood extended to every soul redeemed by the Blood of her Son. She became our comfort, our intercessor, and our companion in suffering.

But why now?

Because this is an age of war — a spiritual war waged not only in culture, but in hearts. And Mary has always been Heaven's secret weapon. She is the one the devil fears most. She crushes the serpent's head — not with might, but with humility; not with argument, but with love.

To return to Mary is not to flee from Christ, but to draw closer to Him. She is the shortcut to holiness, the mirror of His mercy, and the safest refuge for sinners. St. Maximilian Kolbe said, "Never be afraid of loving the Blessed Virgin too much," and "You can never love her more than Jesus did."

This book is not just another collection of meditations. It is an invitation to reparation. A call to console the Hearts of Jesus and Mary — pierced for our sins, yet ablaze with love. It is an opportunity to make your life a Marian offering. To walk the Way of the Cross with her. To see your own wounds reflected in her Sorrows. And to discover, in the silence of her gaze, the strength to carry your own cross.

We live in prophetic times. Times when the triumph of the Immaculate Heart is not merely a promise for the future, but a mission for the present.

May these pages draw you to her side. May they lead you to ponder her sorrows, imitate her courage, and live in the shadow of her maternal love. And as you journey through each reflection, may you hear the whispered invitation that echoes from Calvary:

"Behold your mother."

Chapter 1:
The Prophecy of Simeon
– A Sword Shall Pierce

"And Simeon blessed them and said to Mary his mother, "Behold, this child is set for the fall and rising of many in Israel, and for a sign that is spoken against — (and a sword will pierce through your own soul also), that thoughts out of many hearts may be revealed."

— Luke 2:34–35

The crib and the Cross were never far apart. In the arms of Mary, the Infant Jesus was adored as the Prince of Peace — but in the shadow of Simeon's words, He was already marked as the Man of Sorrows.

This first sorrow of Our Lady is not soaked in blood, yet it is sharp. A sword — invisible, prophetic, and real — is announced. Not for Christ, but for *her*. And this sword, unlike a Roman blade, will not wound the body — it will slice through the heart.

In the Temple, Mary receives more than a blessing. She receives a mission. She is told that her joy in this Child will become sorrow. That the light she holds will also reveal darkness. That her soul, so pure and hidden, will become the mirror in which the drama of redemption is reflected.

The sword is not just pain — it is participation. Mary is being invited into her Son's sufferings. She does not recoil. She does not protest. She receives this word in silence, just as she once received the angel's greeting: *Fiat*.

Archbishop Fulton Sheen once observed that "Mary is the only mother who ever knew she gave birth to a victim." The mystery of Christ's redemptive mission was not revealed to her all at once — but this moment, in the arms of Simeon, begins to unveil it. A sword awaits. And yet, she loves.

In that moment, Mary became the Mother of Sorrows.

A Mother's Heart

To suffer in the body is one thing. To suffer in the heart of a mother is another. Mary's sorrows are not merely emotional; they are *intercessory*. Her pierced soul allows her to enter into the pain of all her children.

Sheen once said, "No one can live without tears unless they have never loved." And Mary loved perfectly. Her heart was open, exposed, undefended —

because her love was pure. That is what made the sword pierce so deeply.

The piercing of Mary's heart reveals something to us: that love and suffering are not opposites. In fact, the deepest love is often the most wounded. But those wounds become fountains of grace. Mary's pierced heart is now a refuge for all broken hearts.

For the Fall and Rise of Many

Simeon speaks of contradiction. He declares that Jesus will be opposed — and so too will His followers. The way of the Cross is never a straight, painless line. It invites a fall — a dying to pride, sin, and self. But it also offers a rising — a resurrection of the soul.

Mary stands at the threshold of this mystery. She accepts that her life will be marked by sorrow, not in despair, but in union with the redeeming plan of God. Her soul becomes a chalice, filled with the pain of the world and the love of the Redeemer.

A Call to Reparation

To meditate on this sorrow is to accept a sword of our own — the sword of compassion, of intercession, of co-suffering. We are invited to stand with Mary in the Temple, to receive the prophecy, and to not turn away.

Her sorrow is not sterile. It is fruitful. And it calls forth a response.

Will you let your own heart be pierced? Will you join her in reparation?

In a world where love is cheap and suffering is avoided, Mary stands as the contradiction. She embraces both.

Let us learn from her how to suffer with grace — and how to love with wounds.

Chapter 2:
The Flight into Egypt
– A Mother's Protection in Exile

*"Now when they had departed, behold, an angel of
the Lord appeared to Joseph in a dream and said,
"Rise, take the child and his mother, and flee to Egypt,
and remain there till I tell you; for Herod is about
to search for the child, to destroy him."*

— Matthew 2:13

The stillness of Bethlehem is shattered by a warning in the night. There is no time to linger. No farewell. No comfort. The Holy Family, newly formed, must become a family in flight — not toward triumph, but into exile.

In the second sorrow of Our Lady, we see a maternal heart full of courage, obedience, and love. She who bore the Light of the world is now forced to flee from darkness. A tyrant wants her Son dead. And so, under cover of night, she sets off — not with fear, but with faith.

Mary does not argue with God. She does not resist the path laid before her. She protects the Child by trusting the Father. And in doing so, she teaches us what it means to guard the Christ-life in our own souls — especially in a world that often seeks to destroy it.

Archbishop Fulton Sheen once noted, *"The modern flight into Egypt takes place when truth is banished from the hearts of men."* In that light, Mary's flight is not just historical — it's mystical. It continues today. Every soul that carries Jesus must make this flight into interior exile, away from sin and toward the Father's will.

The Hidden Heroism of Mothers

The Gospels give us few details of the journey — no distances, no landscapes, no complaints. But what we do know is this: Mary was not simply a mother in distress. She was a mother on a mission.

The dangers were real — robbers, deserts, cold, thirst, uncertainty. But the presence of the Child made every hardship holy. What mother, upon holding the Saviour close, would not give everything for Him?

Mary is the model of mothers who must raise children in difficult times — in spiritual exile, amid moral confusion, under attack from a culture of death. She shows us that the real heroism of motherhood is not found in applause but in quiet sacrifice, made for the sake of protecting what is most sacred.

A Journey of Reparation

Why must the Saviour flee? Why must the Holy Family suffer?

Because even as a Child, Christ is entering into our human condition — the chaos, the evil, the unjust systems. He is the Divine Exile. And Mary, united with Him, begins to offer reparation not just for Herod's cruelty, but for all sin that tries to snuff out divine life.

This is the spiritual meaning of the Flight into Egypt: the refusal to allow the holy to be compromised. The flight is not cowardice; it is fidelity. Mary teaches us when to stand firm and when to flee — not from fear, but from evil.

There are seasons when reparation looks like confrontation. And there are times when it looks like retreat — retreat to prayer, hiddenness, silence. Mary's exile was not wasted time. It was a furnace of love, forged in fidelity.

You, Too, Must Flee

Today, there are many Herods. They come not with swords, but with seductions. They don't burn churches; they distract hearts. They make the soul numb and complacent. And so we are called, like Mary and Joseph, to *flee* — not physically, but spiritually.

To flee from pride.

To flee from impurity.

To flee from anything that would endanger the Christ-life within us.

And we flee not in panic — but in purpose.

Mary is the first of the exiles. The first of the hidden victims. And in her exile, she was never alone. She had the Child. She had Joseph. And above all, she had the will of the Father guiding every step.

Let us journey with her, not only in comfort, but in the desert — where true love is proven, and the soul learns how to make every step an act of reparation.

Chapter 3:
The Loss of the Child Jesus
– When God Hides in Silence

❦

"And when they saw him, they were astonished;
and his mother said to him, 'Son, why have you
treated us so? Behold, your father and I have
been looking for you anxiously."

— *Luke 2:48*

There are few scenes in Scripture more human, more relatable, than this: a mother searching for her lost Child. For three days, Mary and Joseph looked for Jesus, hearts aching with each hour. And when they finally found Him — in the temple, speaking with doctors of the law — her words echoed the cry of every parent, every soul: *Why?*

This sorrow pierces deeply. It is not the suffering of persecution or exile. It is the anguish of silence — the hiddenness of God. Mary, who had never sinned, experiences the pain of not knowing where her Son is. She represents the soul in darkness, the believer in desolation.

Archbishop Fulton Sheen once said, *"It is in the darkness that we find God — the darkness of faith, not of despair."* Mary teaches us that faith endures even when God seems absent. Her sorrow was not a lack of belief — it was the ache of love.

The Silence of the Saints

Saint Thérèse of Lisieux, in her final illness, confessed that her faith was tested not by sin, but by *God's silence*. She, too, lost the sense of His nearness. She, too, cried out in the night. Yet like Mary, she clung to Him with love, not understanding.

There is a silence that purifies. A silence that strips us of superficial devotions, empty feelings, and spiritual pride. In this silence, the soul is asked one question: *Do you love Me still?*

Mary's yes — even in her confusion — teaches us to remain. To search. To keep walking, even when the road grows cold.

Reparation in the Dark

There is a great mystery in this third sorrow: that the One who is Wisdom Itself allows His mother to suffer for love of Him. He does not prevent the loss. He permits it — not out of cruelty, but to deepen her heart.

Reparation is not always about doing. Sometimes it is about *bearing* — bearing the absence, the dryness, the unknowing. These are hidden sufferings, invisible to the world, but precious to God.

To suffer for Christ is holy.

But to suffer from Christ — and still love Him — is divine.

Mary teaches us how to offer the pain of confusion as reparation. She shows us how to pray even when we do not feel God's presence. She is the companion of every soul that walks through the night of faith.

Finding Him Again

When Mary finds Jesus, she does not scold. She questions — gently, sorrowfully — but she does not rebuke the divine plan. And He, in turn, speaks a mystery: *"Did you not know I must be about My Father's business?"*

It is a strange comfort. Not an explanation. But a reminder: that even in absence, Jesus is working. Even when we do not feel Him, He is still fulfilling the Father's will.

Mary pondered all these things in her heart. So must we.

If you feel like you've lost Him —

If your prayers are dry, your soul confused —

If heaven seems quiet and your heart aches with longing — Then this sorrow is yours.

And so is Mary.

Let her lead you back. Not by sight, but by faith. For in the finding — there is not just relief — but a deeper, truer love.

Chapter 4:
Mary Meets Jesus on the Way of the Cross – Love That Does Not Turn Away

"And there followed him a great multitude of the people, and of women, who bewailed and lamented him."

— *Luke 23:27*

No words are recorded between them. No miracles worked. No comfort given.

Just a meeting.

A mother and her Son, locked in a gaze through sweat, blood, and tears, amidst the cruelty of the crowd. On the road to Calvary, Mary does not faint. She does not beg for mercy. She stands. She walks. She *meets* her Son.

And He, bruised and beaten, looks up through swollen eyes… and sees her.

In that moment, love is exchanged without words. A mother's silent yes meets a Son's saving yes. And a sword, once prophesied by Simeon, now cuts deeper than ever.

The Strength of the Mother

Many imagine Mary as frail and soft, but the Gospels show something different. She is strong — strong enough to stand by a condemned Son when others fled. Strong enough to bear witness to His agony. Strong enough to walk with Him, even when it meant walking into suffering.

Archbishop Fulton Sheen wrote:

"It was not a woman who fled at the garden, nor a woman who denied Him at the fire. It was not a woman who stood not beneath the Cross... it was a woman who was faithful."

Mary's strength is not loud or showy. It is the strength of presence — the power of staying.

She did not stop the Cross. She shared it.

The Power of Compassion

The word "compassion" means *to suffer with.* On the road to Calvary, Mary models this perfectly. She does not take Jesus' pain away — she enters it.

In your own life, you will encounter crosses — your own and those of others. Mary's example calls us not to flee, not to fix everything, but to *be present.* To walk with those in sorrow. To love in the midst of pain.

That is reparation: not simply atonement for sin, but love poured out where love was once denied.

When Suffering Meets Suffering

This fourth sorrow is a school of love. Not the love of poetry or sentiment, but of sacrifice. Here we see what it means to love when nothing can be done — except to be near.

Have you met someone on their road of suffering?

Have you stood by a loved one through illness, addiction, loss, or despair?

Have you looked into the eyes of someone you cannot save… and stayed?

Then you know something of this sorrow. You know something of Mary's heart.

Reparation through Presence

Our world fears pain. It turns away from the broken, the dying, the inconvenient. But Mary does not look away. And neither must we.

If we want to console the Heart of Jesus, we must walk His path. We must enter into the mystery of the Cross — not alone, but with Mary.

Stay close to her.

Let her teach you to love without needing answers.

Let her show you that even the smallest act of presence — a hand held, a tear shared, a gaze of love — can redeem.

For when suffering meets suffering in love, Heaven draws near.

Chapter 5:
The Crucifixion
– Standing at the Foot of the Cross

"So the soldiers did this. But standing by the cross of Jesus were his mother, and his mother's sister, Mary the wife of Clopas, and Mary Magdalene."

— John 19:25

It is the most sacred ground in history — Calvary.

And there, as the world looked away in horror, Mary *stood*.

She stood in sorrow, not collapse.

She stood in silence, not protest.

She stood in surrender, not despair.

The Blessed Virgin Mary did not fall at the Cross. She stood *with* the Cross. She stood *under* the Cross. She stood as the Church's first co-sufferer and our model of courageous love.

The Priest and the Woman

As the High Priest offered Himself on the altar of the Cross, a woman offered her heart. Her presence was not incidental; it was integral. She who gave Him flesh now watched that flesh torn apart. She who nursed the infant Christ now beheld Him pierced.

Archbishop Fulton Sheen once wrote:

"Mary at the foot of the Cross is the model of what our attitude should be toward Calvary. She is not a hysterical woman with disheveled hair and sobbing uncontrollably.   She is a strong woman — a queen among women — a queen among martyrs."

Her heart did not break from hopelessness. It broke from love. And that love became the seedbed of reparation.

Behold Your Mother

Only one sentence is recorded from Mary at Calvary — and it is not spoken by her.

It is spoken *to* her.

"Woman, behold, your son!" Then he said to the disciple, "Behold, your mother!"

— John 19:26-27

In that moment, Mary became more than the Mother of Christ — she became the Mother of the Church. The beloved disciple, traditionally understood as John, represents each of us. And to him — to us — Christ entrusts His Mother.

We are not orphans.

We are not alone.

We have been given the greatest advocate and consoler: the Mother of Sorrows.

The Silent Offering

At the foot of the Cross, Mary says nothing. But her silence is not absence. It is *consent*. She offers her Son to the Father, just as she once offered Him in the temple. The world crucifies — she consents. The world mocks — she loves.

This is the heart of reparation: not to undo the world's evil, but to *offer* love in the face of it.

Reparation is not passive. It is deeply active — but the action is interior. It is the prayerful union of our suffering with Christ's. It is the soul whispering, "Fiat," even when the world says, "Crucify."

Our Own Calvaries

There are crosses we are called to *stand beneath*, not run from:

- The sickness of a spouse

- The rebellion of a child

- The grief of a buried dream

- The weight of unanswered prayers

Mary shows us how to stand — not angrily, not hopelessly, but *faithfully*.

She teaches us that presence is power. That fidelity is fruitfulness. That Calvary, endured in union with Christ, is not the end — it is the beginning of Resurrection.

The Call to Stand

To stand at the Cross is to be Catholic.

To stand at the Cross is to be Marian.

To stand at the Cross is to become like Mary: a soul pierced but not defeated.

So stand.

Stand when it's hard.

Stand when it's quiet.

Stand when the world calls you foolish.

For there, at the foot of the Cross, you will find Mary…

And where Mary stands, Heaven is not far behind.

Chapter 6:
The Gift of a Mother
– Marian Love and the Healing of Souls

"If we do not become children, we cannot enter the Kingdom of Heaven. If we do not become Marian, we cannot understand Christ."

— Archbishop Fulton J. Sheen

At the Cross, Jesus gave us His Mother.

He didn't give us doctrine, ritual, or rules — He gave us Mary.

And in doing so, He gave us the most tender path to healing.

Love that Heals

Marian love is not a sentimental devotion. It is a *healing encounter*. Mary's love heals not by replacing the Cross, but by guiding us through it. She walks with the wounded. She consoles the broken. She mothers the sinners.

Her heart — immaculate and pierced — has room for every soul.

Just as she wrapped the Christ-Child in swaddling clothes, she now wraps us in the folds of her mantle. She does not take away suffering. She walks us into the fire — and out of it — as only a mother can.

Reparation Is Womb-Like

Reparation in union with Mary becomes a *birthing place* of grace. She teaches us to suffer not with bitterness but with fruitfulness.

Think of the womb: silent, hidden, sacrificial. A mother's body makes space for another — and in doing so, she co-creates life.

This is Marian reparation.

We create space in our hearts to carry the pain of others. We make of our trials a tabernacle. And in silence, in surrender, in trust — love is born again.

The Devotion of the Little Ones

St. Thérèse of Lisieux, child of Mary and Doctor of the Church, called Mary "more Mother than Queen." For St. Thérèse, it was the *simplicity* of Mary that made her powerful. Mary was not distant or unapproachable, but tender, motherly, and near.

St. Thérèse wrote:

"She is so simple, that one cannot fear her."

Do you fear approaching God?

Are you ashamed of your past, your wounds, your weakness?

Go to Mary.

She will not turn you away. She will teach you to walk the Little Way — a path of confidence, childlike surrender, and humble trust.

The Mission of a Mother

Every soul wounded by sin is a soul waiting to be mothered. Every person drifting in spiritual confusion is silently aching for a maternal hand. And every Church — even in her majesty and sacraments — needs the tenderness of a Mother to be complete.

Mary is not a footnote in salvation history. She is the living heart of the Church.

To be Marian is to become fully alive.

To be Marian is to know how to suffer well.

To be Marian is to receive love so deeply that we cannot help but give it away.

Entrustment and Healing

When we entrust our pain to Mary, we do not lose it — we *offer* it. She gathers our broken pieces and places them, like little flowers, at the foot of the Cross.

And there, with tears and trust, Heaven transforms them.

So go ahead — bring your wounds to the Mother.

- Bring your guilt.

- Bring your fatigue.

- Bring your unspoken ache.

She will not condemn.

She will not reject.

She will carry you as she carried Christ — all the way to the Resurrection.

Chapter 7:
The Immaculate Heart and the Wounded Heart

In every image of Our Lady of Sorrows, we see two hearts in profound dialogue — her Immaculate Heart, pure and sinless, and the Wounded Heart of her Son, pierced for our salvation. This mystery is not only artistic but deeply theological: the two hearts beat in unison, sharing the same love for the Father, the same sorrow for sin, and the same longing for our redemption.

Mary's Heart was fashioned to be the perfect echo of Jesus' Heart. If His Sacred Heart burned with divine charity, hers burned with maternal charity. If His Heart was pierced by the lance on Calvary, hers was pierced mystically at that very moment by a sword foretold by Simeon. She did not merely witness His Passion; she interiorly suffered it with Him. This co-suffering, called *compassio* by the saints, is not a claim of equality with the Redeemer, but of intimate participation in His work.

Archbishop Fulton Sheen often spoke of Mary as "the only one who truly understood the cost of our salvation." She had no illusions about the price of sin. She held the Innocent Lamb at Bethlehem; she watched Him grow in wisdom and stature; she saw Him rejected by the very ones He came to save. And then she stood at the foot of the Cross — the place where the price was fully paid.

St. Thérèse of Lisieux, though so tender in her love for the Child Jesus, also grasped the sorrow of Mary. In her simple yet profound way, she wrote:

"Mary is more Mother than Queen; her glory is not in power but in tenderness, not in majesty but in mercy."

Mary's compassion was not a passing sentiment; it was the fruit of perfect love. She teaches us that to truly love Christ means to suffer with Him and for Him. The Immaculate Heart beats for sinners, not because sin is light, but because grace is greater. Her maternal mission did not end at Calvary — it intensified. From the Cross, Jesus entrusted John to Mary and Mary to John. In that moment, she became Mother to every disciple.

The woundedness of her Heart is, paradoxically, the source of her power. The devil fears Mary because she shares so perfectly in the victory of her Son. Her Immaculate Heart is a refuge for the repentant, a fortress for the weak, and a beacon for the wandering. Devotion to her Heart is not a sentimental exercise but a school of sacrificial love.

To honor the Immaculate Heart is to join Mary in contemplating the wounds of Jesus — not with cold observation, but with loving participation. We place our hearts within hers so that she may shape them according to the Heart of her Son. And in this exchange, we learn to say with her: "Behold the Handmaid of the Lord; be it done unto me according to thy word."

Chapter 8:
Mary at the Foot of the Cross:
The School of Love and Suffering

No scene in all of human history reveals the depth of love and the cost of redemption more than Calvary. At the foot of the Cross stands Mary, the Mother of Jesus, steadfast and silent, her soul pierced with the sword foretold by Simeon. It is here, in this hour of darkness, that she becomes for us the model of unwavering faith, total surrender, and selfless love.

Archbishop Fulton Sheen often remarked that *"Mary's greatest moment was not in Bethlehem when she gave birth to Christ, but on Calvary when she gave Him up."* In Bethlehem, she offered Him her body; on Calvary, she offered Him her heart. Here we enter the mystery of the union between a Mother's love and a Redeemer's mission.

The Gaze of the Mother

The Gospels give us no recorded words from Mary at the Cross. Her silence speaks more loudly than any speech. Her eyes were fixed on Jesus, absorbing His pain into her heart, uniting her soul with His sacrifice. She did not turn away. She did not despair. Her steadfast presence teaches us the ministry of accompaniment — to be present with those who suffer, even when we cannot remove their pain.

In our own trials, how often do we look away from the Cross, seeking easier paths? Mary's gaze invites us to remain — to stand at the place of suffering with courage and fidelity. To see with her eyes is to see suffering through the lens of love.

The Gift of Spiritual Motherhood

From the Cross, Jesus utters words that change the course of salvation history: *"Woman, behold your son."* And to St. John: *"Behold your mother."* In that moment, Mary becomes the Mother of all the redeemed. She takes into her heart every soul purchased by the Blood of Christ. Fulton Sheen notes that Mary's spiritual motherhood is not a vague sentiment, but a deep participation in the redemptive mission of her Son. She mothers us into holiness, nurturing Christ's life in our souls.

The School of Love and Suffering

To stand with Mary at the Cross is to enroll in the school of love and suffering. Here we learn that love without sacrifice is shallow, and suffering without love is unbearable. In her school, suffering becomes fruitful when united to Christ's Passion. She teaches us to offer our pain — whether physical, emotional, or spiritual — as a gift to God for the salvation of souls.

Saint Thérèse of Lisieux, who bore the title *"of the Child Jesus and the Holy Face"*, learned this Marian lesson well. Her "little way" was filled with small sacrifices offered with great love, echoing Mary's quiet yet powerful "yes" beneath the Cross.

Remaining at the Foot of the Cross Today

Mary's example is not confined to history. In our own times of trial, we are called to "remain" with Christ in the Eucharist, in Adoration, and in prayer. To kneel at the tabernacle is to kneel at Calvary, where Mary still invites us to behold her Son and allow His love to transform us.

The world seeks comfort without cost, love without commitment, and faith without the Cross. Mary reminds us that there is no Easter Sunday without Good Friday. She leads us to embrace the Cross not as a sign of defeat, but as the tree of victory.

Chapter 9:
Mary at the Foot of the Cross:
The Perfect Model of Reparation

The Gospels tell us that "standing by the cross of Jesus were His mother, and His mother's sister, Mary the wife of Clopas, and Mary Magdalene" (John 19:25). At the most excruciating moment in human history, when the weight of the world's sins bore down upon the Saviour, Mary did not turn away. She stood. She remained. She endured.

This standing was no passive stance. It was the posture of unwavering fidelity, of full union with the redemptive suffering of her Son. She was not merely present as an onlooker — Mary was actively participating in the offering of Christ to the Father. Every mother suffers when her child suffers; yet Mary's suffering was unique because she consented, with the deepest act of her will, to the sacrifice unfolding before her.

Saint John Paul II described her as "co-suffering" with Christ. This does not diminish the unique role of Jesus as the Redeemer — rather, it shows the depth of Mary's maternal union with Him. She accepted in advance the piercing of her own soul, prophesied by Simeon, and when it came, she embraced it as her share in the redemption of mankind.

Archbishop Fulton Sheen would often say that Mary's greatest title is not merely "Mother of God," but "Mother of the Redeemer." The difference is subtle yet profound. As "Mother of God," she gave Jesus His humanity. As "Mother of the Redeemer," she joined herself to His mission, offering her will, her love, and her suffering in complete harmony with His.

In the mystery of reparation, Mary becomes our teacher. She shows us that reparation is not simply saying prayers of apology for sin—it is uniting ourselves to Christ's sacrifice in such a way that our lives become an offering of love to the Father. This means standing with Jesus in the moments of darkness, humiliation, and abandonment, and choosing not to run from the Cross.

In our own lives, this can take many forms: standing by a suffering family member, refusing to abandon our faith in moments of trial, or offering our hidden sufferings in silence for souls in need. When we do so with Mary at our side, we share in her steadfast love and unshakable fidelity.

At Calvary, Mary became the spiritual mother of all who would follow her Son. From the Cross, Jesus entrusted her to John—and through John, to us. We who take her into our hearts are invited to share in her mission of bringing souls to Christ through the power of reparation.

Reflection Questions:

1) When have you felt called to "stand by the Cross" in your own life?

2) How can you imitate Mary's unwavering presence in the face of suffering?

3) What specific acts of reparation can you offer this week for the conversion of souls?

Prayer:

O Sorrowful Mother, who stood with courage and love beside your crucified Son, teach me to stand faithfully in the shadow of the Cross. May my life be a living act of reparation, united to the Heart of Jesus and to your Immaculate Heart. Amen.

Chapter 10:
Mary at the Foot of the Cross:
The Model of Perseverance in Suffering

The scene at Calvary is the ultimate classroom of love, perseverance, and faith.

Here, at the foot of the Cross, stands Mary — silent, steadfast, unyielding in her fidelity. While others fled, she remained. While many despaired, she trusted. In her heart, sorrow and faith met in a mysterious embrace.

St. John's Gospel gives us the briefest description:

"Standing by the cross of Jesus were his mother, and his mother's sister, Mary the wife of Clopas, and Mary Magdalene"
John 19:25

The brevity of the verse almost hides the depth of the reality — but in that single image, the Church has found endless inspiration for centuries.

1. Perseverance: The Fruit of Love

Mary did not endure this suffering out of mere obligation; she remained because her love for God was greater than the pain of the moment. In this, she shows us that perseverance is not rooted in stoicism, but in love.

Fulton Sheen once said, *"When love enters the soul, pain no longer remains pain; it becomes sacrifice."* Mary understood this truth perfectly.

2. The Silence of the Suffering

At Calvary, Mary's silence speaks volumes. She does not argue with the soldiers, nor cry out in protest. Her silence is not resignation, but a deep participation in the mystery unfolding before her eyes.

In our own trials, there are moments when silence becomes the most eloquent prayer — a silent offering of self to God.

3. A Call to Remain

In the spiritual life, perseverance is often the hardest virtue to maintain. It is easy to begin with enthusiasm; it is another thing entirely to remain faithful when the Cross becomes heavy. Mary teaches us to *remain* — not because the suffering is bearable, but because God is worthy.

When your spiritual journey brings you to your own Calvary — whether in illness, misunderstanding, loss, or spiritual dryness — remember Mary's example. She stayed, even when she could not fully see the glory that was to come.

4. The Gift She Received

At the Cross, Mary was entrusted with the whole human family through the words of Jesus:

"'Woman, behold, your son!" Then he said to the disciple, "Behold, your mother!" And from that hour the disciple took her to his own home."

John 19:26–27

In persevering, she received a new mission — to be Mother to every disciple. This is the hidden blessing of remaining faithful: in our endurance, God often entrusts us with a deeper calling.

Reflection:

In moments of trial, ask Our Lady to help you stand with her at the foot of the Cross. Let her steadfastness inspire your own. The Cross is not the end — it is the doorway to Resurrection.

Prayer:

O Mary, faithful Mother, teach me to remain at the foot of my crosses with you. When I am tempted to flee, give me the courage to stay. When I am tempted to despair, whisper to my heart the hope of the Resurrection. Amen.

Chapter 11:
The Compassion of Mary at the Foot of the Cross

No human heart has ever shared in the sufferings of Christ as deeply as the Immaculate Heart of His Mother. At Calvary, Mary stood—silent, steadfast, and sorrowful—bearing in her soul the full weight of her Son's agony. She did not cry out in despair, nor did she collapse in grief. She stood. And by standing, she revealed the strength of her faith and the depth of her love.

Saint John tells us simply: *"Standing by the Cross of Jesus was His Mother"* (John 19:25). That short phrase contains a world of meaning. Mary's presence was not a passive one. Her standing was an act of courage, an offering of herself in union with her Son's redemptive sacrifice. She was the New Eve at the side of the New Adam, sharing in the victory over sin and death.

Archbishop Fulton Sheen once said that Mary's greatest suffering was not the sword in her own heart, but watching the sword pierce the Heart of her Son. Every lash, every jeer, every drop of blood was felt in her soul. She was the most faithful disciple, the one who believed without seeing, who trusted even when all seemed lost.

Her compassion was not mere emotion — it was participation. In her, we see what it means to take up the Cross, to stand firm in faith when trials press in. The Church calls her *Co-Redemptrix* not because she adds to the work of Christ, but because she shares in it uniquely and completely, giving her maternal "Yes" even when it costs her everything.

For us, the lesson is clear: if we wish to draw near to Christ in His Passion, we must draw near to Mary. She teaches us how to suffer with love, how to unite our pain to His, and how to remain faithful in the darkest hour.

Reflection Question:

When I stand at the foot of the Cross — in my own trials or in those of others — do I waver, or do I remain steadfast with Mary?

Prayer:

O Mother of Sorrows, teach me to stand with you at the foot of the Cross, to love Jesus with a faithful heart, and to offer my own sufferings in union with His for the salvation of souls. Amen.

Chapter 12:
The Seven Sorrows and
the Power of Reparation

Mary's life was marked by joy, but also by a deep sharing in the sufferings of her Son. The Church, in her wisdom, has given us the devotion of the **Seven Sorrows of Mary** so we may meditate upon the mysteries that pierced her Immaculate Heart:

1) The Prophecy of Simeon
2) The Flight into Egypt
3) The Loss of the Child Jesus in the Temple
4) Meeting Jesus on the Way to Calvary
5) The Crucifixion and Death of Jesus
6) The Taking Down of the Body of Jesus from the Cross
7) The Burial of Jesus

Each sorrow is a window into the heart of the Mother of God. In everyone, she responds not with resentment but with love, accepting the will of the Father even when it is shrouded in mystery and pain.

In meditating on her sorrows, we enter into the school of reparation. Mary teaches us how to atone—not by adding to Christ's sacrifice, but by uniting ourselves to it with love. Fulton Sheen wrote: *"The closer one gets to Mary, the more one sees that her life was a continual Calvary."*

Reparation is not simply making amends; it is love's response to wounded love. Our sins have wounded the Heart of Jesus, and through Him, the Heart of Mary. By offering our prayers, sacrifices, and daily crosses in union with hers, we participate in the healing work of grace.

One of the most fruitful ways to live this devotion is to set aside time each week — especially on Fridays — to meditate upon the Seven Sorrows. As we do, we find that Mary's sorrows are not sources of despair, but of hope, because they lead directly to the Resurrection.

Reflection Question:

How can I imitate Mary's faith in times of sorrow so that my suffering becomes a prayer of love?

Prayer:

O Mother most sorrowful, obtain for me the grace to unite my heart to yours, that I may console the Heart of your Son and help bring souls to His mercy. Amen.

Chapter 13:
Mary as Mother of the Church and of Our Mission

At the foot of the Cross, Jesus gave us His Mother: *"Behold your mother"* (John 19:27). These were not words for John alone — they were for all of us. In that moment, Mary became the Mother of the Church, the Mother of every believer, the Mother of our mission.

As Mother of the Church, she prays for us, guides us, and nurtures us in the life of grace. As Mother of our mission, she leads us into the heart of her Son's work: the salvation of souls. She does not keep us for herself but sends us out, as she did the servants at Cana, with the command: *"Do whatever He tells you."*

In every age of the Church, Mary has raised up apostles, missionaries, and saints who bring Christ to the world. From the shepherd children of Fatima to the humble Carmelite of Lisieux, she has shown that God chooses the little ones to confound the strong. She wants to do the same with us.

If we allow her to, Mary will form us into true disciples — men and women of prayer, courage, and charity — capable of standing at the foot of the Cross and of carrying it into the world. She will teach us the humility that attracts grace and the boldness that proclaims the Gospel without fear.

Our mission, then, is inseparable from hers: to lead souls to Jesus. Whether in the quiet of a hidden life or the bustle of public ministry, we are called to live as children of Mary, loving Christ as she loves Him, serving others as she serves, and trusting always in God's plan.

Reflection Question:

How is Mary inviting me to participate more fully in the mission of the Church today?

Prayer:

Mary, Mother of the Church, guide my steps, strengthen my faith, and help me to bring Christ to every soul I meet. Amen.

Chapter 14
Quotes from Archbishop Fulton J. Sheen and St. Thérèse of Lisieux

Archbishop Fulton J. Sheen Speaks

"Mary is not only the Mother of Jesus, but she is the Mother of all those who follow Him. At Bethlehem, she gave birth to the Head; at Calvary, she became the Mother of the Body."

"The closer one comes to Mary, the more one becomes like her Son, for her whole mission is to magnify Him."

"Mary teaches us to stand at the Cross not in bitterness, but in love – seeing even in suffering the shadow of the Resurrection."

"The Mother of Jesus is the quickest, surest, and easiest way to the Heart of her Son."

St. Thérèse of Lisieux Speaks

"She is more Mother than Queen."

"Mary is more a Mother than a Queen, for she loves us and knows our weakness."

"It is the Blessed Virgin who, having lived in obscurity, teaches me how to serve God in the hiddenness of everyday life."

"With Mary, I will stay near the Cross, and with her, I will rise in the joy of Easter."

Chapter 15:
Scripture Reflections for the Holy Hour

These passages are offered for prayer and meditation during a Holy Hour of Reparation, especially in union with the Blessed Virgin Mary at the Cross.

Old Testament

Isaiah 7:14

Therefore, the Lord himself will give you a sign. Behold, a young woman shall conceive and bear a son and shall call his name Immanuel.

Isaiah 53:3–5

He was despised and rejected by men; a man of sorrows, and acquainted with grief; and as one from whom men hide their faces he was despised, and we esteemed him not.
Surely he has borne our griefs and carried our sorrows; yet we esteemed him stricken, smitten by God, and afflicted.

But he was wounded for our transgressions, he was bruised for our iniquities; upon him was the chastisement that made us whole, and with his stripes we are healed.

Lamentations 1:12

Is it nothing to you, all you who pass by? Look and see if there is any sorrow like my sorrow which was brought upon me, which the Lord inflicted on the day of his fierce anger.

Zechariah 12:10

And I will pour out on the house of David and the inhabitants of Jerusalem a spirit of compassion and supplication, so that, when they look on him whom they have pierced, they shall mourn for him, as one mourns for an only child, and weep bitterly over him, as one weeps over a first-born.

Gospels

Luke 1:26–38 – The Birth of Jesus Foretold

In the sixth month the angel Gabriel was sent from God to a city of Galilee named Nazareth, to a virgin betrothed to a man whose name was Joseph, of the house of David; and the virgin's name was Mary. And he came to her and said, "Hail, full of grace, the Lord is with you!" But she was greatly troubled at the saying, and considered in her mind what sort of greeting this might be. And the angel said to her, "Do not be afraid, Mary, for you have found favor with God. And behold, you will conceive in your womb and bear a son, and you shall call his name Jesus.

He will be great, and will be called the Son of the Most High; and the Lord God will give to him the throne of his father David, and he will reign over the house of Jacob for ever; and of his kingdom there will be no end."

And Mary said to the angel, "How can this be, since I have no husband?"

And the angel said to her,
"The Holy Spirit will come upon you,
and the power of the Most High will overshadow you;
therefore the child to be born will be called holy,
the Son of God.

And behold, your kinswoman Elizabeth in her old age has also conceived a son; and this is the sixth month with her who was called barren. For with God nothing will be impossible." And Mary said, "Behold, I am the handmaid of the Lord; let it be to me according to your word." And the angel departed from her.

Luke 2:25–35 – The Prophecy of Simeon

Now there was a man in Jerusalem, whose name was Simeon, and this man was righteous and devout, looking for the consolation of Israel, and the Holy Spirit was upon him.

And it had been revealed to him by the Holy Spirit that he should not see death before he had seen the Lord's Christ.

And inspired by the Spirit he came into the temple; and when the parents brought in the child Jesus, to do for him according to the custom of the law, he took him up in his arms and blessed God and said,

"Lord, now lettest thou thy servant depart in peace, according to thy word; for mine eyes have seen thy salvation which thou hast prepared in the presence of all peoples, a light for revelation to the Gentiles, and for glory to thy people Israel."

And his father and his mother marveled at what was said about him; and Simeon blessed them and said to Mary his mother,

"Behold, this child is set for the fall and rising of many in Israel, and for a sign that is spoken against (and a sword will pierce through your own soul also),
that thoughts out of many hearts may be revealed."

John 2:1–11 – The Wedding at Cana

On the third day there was a marriage at Cana in Galilee, and the mother of Jesus was there; Jesus also was invited to the marriage, with his disciples. When the wine failed, the mother of Jesus said to him, "They have no wine." And Jesus said to her, "O woman, what have you to do with me? My hour has not yet come." His mother said to the servants, "Do whatever he tells you." Now six stone jars were standing there, for the Jewish rites of purification, each holding twenty or thirty gallons. Jesus said to them, "Fill the jars with water." And they filled them up to the brim. He said to them, "Now draw some out, and take it to the steward of the feast." So they took it. When the steward of the feast tasted the water now become wine, and did not know where it came from (though the servants who had drawn the water knew), the steward of the feast called the bridegroom and said to him, "Every man serves the good wine first; and when men have drunk freely, then the poor wine; but you have kept the good wine until now." This, the first of his signs, Jesus did at Cana in Galilee, and manifested his glory; and his disciples believed in him.

John 19:25-27 – Mary at the Foot of the Cross

So the soldiers did this. But standing by the cross of Jesus were his mother, and his mother's sister, Mary the wife of Clopas, and Mary Magdalene. When Jesus saw his mother, and the disciple whom he loved standing near, he said to his mother, "Woman, behold, your son!" Then he said to the disciple, "Behold, your mother!" And from that hour the disciple took her to his own home.

Acts & Epistles

Acts 1:14

All these with one accord devoted themselves to prayer, together with the women and Mary the mother of Jesus, and with his brethren.

Galatians 4:4-5

But when the time had fully come, God sent forth his Son, born of woman, born under the law, to redeem those who were under the law, so that we might receive adoption as sons.

Hebrews 12:1-3 - The Example of Jesus

Therefore, since we are surrounded by so great a cloud of witnesses, let us also lay aside every weight, and sin which clings so closely, and let us run with perseverance the race that is set before us, looking to Jesus the pioneer and perfecter of our faith, who for the joy that was set before him endured the cross, despising the shame, and is seated at the right hand of the throne of God. Consider him who endured from sinners such hostility against himself, so that you may not grow weary or fainthearted.

Chapter 16:
How to Begin Your Own
Holy Hour of Reparation

A Holy Hour of Reparation is more than a devotional practice — it is an intimate encounter with the Heart of Jesus through the Heart of Mary. In *Behold Your Mother*, we are invited to make this hour in union with Our Blessed Mother, who stood faithfully at the foot of the Cross.

Just as St. John welcomed Mary into his home (John 19:27), we welcome her into our prayer. She becomes our model and companion in making reparation to the Sacred Heart of Jesus, especially for the sins and indifference committed against Him.

1. Preparing for the Hour

I. Choose the time and place. Ideally, make your Holy Hour before the Blessed Sacrament, exposed or reserved in the tabernacle. If this is not possible, set aside a quiet space in your home with a crucifix and an image of Our Lady.

II. Bring your spiritual aids. A Rosary, Holy Scriptures, a prayer book, and any Marian devotions (such as the Seven Sorrows or the Litany of Loreto).

III. Unite your intention with Mary's. Begin by asking the Blessed Mother to lend you her heart so that you may love Jesus with her purity, faith, and unwavering fidelity.

2. Structure of the Hour

While the Holy Spirit may guide you differently from time to time, the following structure can help:

a) Opening Act of Consecration

Offer yourself entirely to Jesus through Mary, acknowledging her as the perfect guide in reparation and intercession.

b) Scripture and Meditation

Read a passage that draws you into the mystery of Mary at the Cross — such as John 19:25-27 or Luke 2:34-35. Meditate on how her Immaculate Heart suffered in union with her Son.

c) Prayer of Reparation

Offer prayers specifically in atonement for sins against the Sacred Heart of Jesus and the Immaculate Heart of Mary — blasphemies, neglect, sacrilege, and indifference.

d) Marian Devotion

Pray the Rosary or the Seven Sorrows in a spirit of reparation, uniting each mystery to Mary's participation in Christ's saving work.

e) Silent Adoration

Spend a few moments simply gazing at Jesus — through the eyes of Mary. Ask her to help you listen to His voice and console His Heart.

f) Closing Act of Praise and Thanksgiving

Thank Jesus and Mary for the grace of this hour. Offer it for the Church, for priests, for sinners, and for the triumph of the Immaculate Heart.

3. Perseverance in the Practice

1) Choose a regular time. Whether weekly or daily, faithfulness deepens the grace of reparation.

2) Invite Mary into each Hour. Begin every Holy Hour by placing yourself in her hands, asking her to shape your prayer as she shaped her own at Calvary.

3) Offer your trials as prayer. Unite your sufferings — great or small — to the Cross, placing them into Mary's hands as a bouquet for Jesus.

"To Jesus through Mary — there is no surer path, no more perfect way to console His Heart."

Chapter 17:
Fulton Sheen's Holy Hour Reflections

1. Why Make a Holy Hour with Mary?

There are as many reasons for making a Holy Hour as there are souls who love Jesus. The essential reason is this: **love seeks company.** When you love someone, you wish to be near them — not only to speak, but to listen, to gaze, to be silent together.

The Blessed Mother understood this perfectly. She spent thirty years in the hidden life with her Son, treasuring every word and every gesture in her Immaculate Heart (Luke 2:19). At Calvary, she kept her place beside Him even when the world turned away. Your Holy Hour is a continuation of that Marian faithfulness — standing spiritually beside the Cross.

Our Lord asked, *"Could you not watch one hour with Me?"* (Matthew 26:40). Mary answered that call with her whole life. To make a Holy Hour is to join her in consoling the Heart of Christ — adoring Him, loving Him, and offering reparation for the coldness and ingratitude He still receives.

Fulton Sheen wrote:

"The purpose of the Holy Hour is to encourage a deep personal encounter with Christ. It is not an hour of lecturing, but of loving; not of talking, but of listening; not of reading, but of adoring."

When your Holy Hour is made *with Mary*, she teaches you how to listen deeply. She whispers in your heart the words she once said at Cana: *"Do whatever He tells you"* (John 2:5).

In the world's eyes, an hour spent in quiet adoration may seem unproductive. But in Heaven's view, that hour — offered with Mary — is rich beyond measure. Sheen often said that the world is not dying from lack of work, but from lack of prayer. If more souls would unite themselves to Christ in the Eucharist with Mary, there would be more strength for the Church, more holiness among priests, more conversions among sinners, and more peace in the world.

The Holy Hour is also a powerful **act of reparation**. The Immaculate Heart of Mary still suffers because her Son is wounded by indifference and sin. When you kneel in adoration and pray with her, you are helping to console both Hearts — offering love where there has been coldness, fidelity where there has been betrayal, and hope where there has been despair.

"To watch one hour with Jesus, in the company of Mary, is to repair a thousand hours of the world's forgetfulness."

2. How to Make a Holy Hour with Mary

There is no single formula for making a Holy Hour, but the saints teach us that certain dispositions open the soul most fully to grace. When you make a Holy Hour **with Mary**, it becomes not only your prayer, but *hers* — and she presents it, adorned with her purity and love, to her Son.

Begin with Presence

Enter the church or chapel with a Marian heart. Remember how Mary approached her Son at Cana — with confidence, reverence, and love. Genuflect slowly, consciously, as if you were greeting Him in person — because you are.

Sheen often encouraged beginning the hour by **offering it in reparation** — for your own sins, for those of your family, for priests, and for the whole Church. Mary's Immaculate Heart will join your intention to hers, making it pleasing to the Sacred Heart of Jesus.

"Through Mary, we go to Jesus more quickly, more gently, and more perfectly." — St. Louis de Montfort

A Suggested Structure

You may divide the hour into three parts — though Mary may inspire you to linger in one part longer than another:

1) Adoration and Love – Simply gaze upon the Eucharistic Face of Jesus. You may pray silently:

"Lord Jesus, I am here with Your Mother. Look upon me as You looked upon her at Calvary." Let Mary help you adore, just as she adored Him in Bethlehem, in Nazareth, and at the Cross.

2) Reparation and Intercession – Speak to Him of the wounds of His Church and of the world. Offer your own heart, united with Mary's, to repair for sin. Use prayers like the **Chaplet of the Holy Face** or the **Seven Sorrows of Mary**.

3) Listening and Union – Be still. Allow His words to echo in your heart, as they did in Mary's. She will teach you to ponder, to treasure, and to surrender.

Scripture with Mary

Reading the Gospels during a Holy Hour can be especially fruitful when seen through Mary's eyes. For example:

I. At the **Annunciation** (Luke 1:26–38), contemplate her "yes" and ask for the grace to say your own.

II. At the **Visitation** (Luke 1:39–56), join her in bringing Christ's presence to others.

III. At the **Cross** (John 19:25–27), receive her anew as your Mother.

End with Thanksgiving

Before leaving, thank Jesus for the gift of this hour and thank Mary for leading you into His presence. Sheen advised making a simple resolution to carry a grace from the hour into your daily life — perhaps more patience, more charity, or a deeper devotion to Our Lady.

Leave quietly, carrying in your soul the peace Mary always leaves behind.

"A Holy Hour in the presence of the Eucharist is worth more than a thousand sermons." — Fulton J. Sheen.

When made with Mary, it becomes even more — a rehearsal for eternity, when we will adore Him forever with her.

Appendix I:
Marian Rosaries & Special Chaplets

MARIAN ROSARY OF REPARATION (Version 1)

Historical Introduction

The Rosary of Reparation is a powerful spiritual weapon for healing the wounds inflicted upon the Sacred Heart of Jesus and the Immaculate Heart of Mary by sin, sacrilege, and indifference.

In this Marian-focused form, each decade is prayed not only in honor of the mysteries of Christ's life, death, and resurrection, but also in union with Mary — the first and most perfect disciple — who stood at the foot of the Cross and continues to intercede for the world.

This devotion unites us with her maternal mission of reparation, echoing her call at Fatima to "pray the Rosary every day for the conversion of sinners" and to console the Hearts of Jesus and Mary.

How to Pray the Rosary of Reparation

1. Begin with the Sign of the Cross.
2. Pray the Apostles' Creed, Our Father, three Hail Marys (for Faith, Hope, and Charity), and the Glory Be.
3. For each decade:
4. Announce the Mystery.
5. Read the Marian-focused meditation.
6. Pray 1 Our Father, 10 Hail Marys, and 1 Glory Be.
7. Conclude with the Hail Holy Queen and the Prayer of Reparation.

Mysteries & Meditations

The Joyful Mysteries

The Annunciation

Mary's humble "Fiat" opens the way for our salvation. We join her in offering our whole selves to God's will in reparation for pride and disobedience in the world. *(Luke 1:26–38).*

O Virgin Mary, chosen before all ages to be the Mother of God, you listened with a humble and open heart to the angel's message. In your "Fiat," we see the model of perfect surrender to the will of God. We unite our hearts to yours, offering reparation for every refusal of God's plan, and for every soul that resists His grace. May your "Yes" echo in our hearts and draw us into perfect obedience to the Father.

Reparation Offering: We offer this decade for all who resist God's call to holiness.

The Visitation

Mary brings Christ to Elizabeth, radiating joy. We offer reparation for the failure to bring Christ to others in word and deed. *(Luke 1:39–56)*

Mary, bearer of the Word made flesh, you went in haste to serve your cousin Elizabeth, bringing Christ to her home. In your footsteps, we learn that love cannot wait, and that charity is the overflow of grace. We offer reparation for selfishness and indifference toward the needs of others, especially toward the poor, the sick, and the forgotten. Teach us to bring Jesus to every soul we meet, as you did in that joyful encounter.

Reparation Offering: We offer this decade for the conversion of hearts closed to the suffering of others.

The Nativity

In poverty and humility, Christ is born. We make reparation for materialism and indifference to the poor. *(Luke 2:1–20)*

Mary, you brought forth the Light of the world in the stillness of Bethlehem's night. The King of Kings lay in poverty, and heaven rejoiced while earth slept. We offer reparation for the rejection of the Christ Child in our times — in hearts, in homes, and in nations that have turned from Him. As we kneel beside you at the manger, we ask for hearts that welcome Christ without reserve.

Reparation Offering: We offer this decade for those who do not recognize or adore Jesus in the Eucharist.

The Presentation in the Temple

Mary and Joseph offer Jesus to the Father. We offer reparation for neglect of God's law and the rejection of His gifts. *(Luke 2:22–38)*

Mary, you carried your Son to the Temple, offering Him to the Father and submitting to the law in perfect obedience. Simeon's prophecy revealed that your soul would be pierced by a sword. We offer reparation for the disobedience and rebellion found in the world today, and for every refusal to honor God's law. Help us to surrender our lives into God's hands as you and Joseph did that day.

Reparation Offering: We offer this decade for those who resist God's commandments and reject His authority.

The Finding in the Temple

Mary and Joseph find Jesus after days of sorrow. We offer reparation for those who wander from the faith and for lukewarm souls. *(Luke 2:41–52)*

Mary, after days of sorrow, you found your Son in the Temple, teaching and revealing His mission. Your heart was filled with relief and joy, yet you pondered His words in silence. We offer reparation for the loss of faith in countless souls and for those who search for meaning in places where God is not found. May we always seek and find Jesus in the house of the Father and never stray from His presence.

Reparation Offering: We offer this decade for those who have lost their faith and for their return to the Church.

The Luminous Mysteries

The Baptism of Jesus

Christ is revealed as the Beloved Son. We offer reparation for the rejection of baptismal grace. *(Matthew 3:13–17)*

Mary, you stood unseen but close to your Son as He began His public ministry in the waters of the Jordan. In His baptism, He sanctified the waters for our rebirth in the Spirit. We offer reparation for the rejection of baptism, for those who delay or neglect the sacrament, and for the loss of the sense of its grace. Mother, help us to live our baptismal vows with renewed fidelity.

Reparation Offering: We offer this decade for those who have been baptized but live far from the life of grace.

The Wedding at Cana

Mary intercedes for the couple in need. We make reparation for the breakdown of family life. *(John 2:1–12)*

Mary, at Cana, you noticed the needs of the newlyweds and interceded for them, prompting your Son's first miracle. Your motherly heart is always attentive to our needs, especially when our spiritual joy runs dry. We offer reparation for those who reject your intercession or who doubt your maternal care. Help us to obey your counsel, "Do whatever He tells you, "In all things.

Reparation Offering: We offer this decade for couples and families in need of healing and unity.

The Proclamation of the Kingdom

Jesus calls all to repentance. We offer reparation for stubbornness in sin. *(Mark 1:14–15)*

Mary, you heard your Son preach the good news of the Kingdom and call sinners to repentance. You rejoiced when the lost were found and the wounded healed. We offer reparation for the hardness of heart that refuses to repent, for the pride that rejects God's mercy, and for the spreading of false teachings that obscure the truth of Christ's Kingdom.

Reparation Offering: We offer this decade for the conversion of sinners and the triumph of truth.

The Transfiguration

Jesus is revealed in glory. We make reparation for failure to believe in His divinity. *(Matthew 17:1–9)*

Mary, you were not present on Mount Tabor, yet you believed without seeing the glory revealed to Peter, James, and John. Your life was a constant "yes" to the mystery of your Son's divinity. We offer reparation for disbelief in Christ's divinity and for irreverence toward the sacred. Help us to behold Jesus with the eyes of faith and to be transformed by His light.

Reparation Offering: We offer this decade for those who doubt or deny the divinity of Jesus.

The Institution of the Eucharist

Christ gives us His Body and Blood. We offer reparation for sacrilege and neglect of the Blessed Sacrament. *(Luke 22:14–20)*

Mary, you gave the world the Flesh and Blood of your Son, and at the Last Supper, He gave Himself to us forever in the Holy Eucharist. We offer reparation for every sacrilege, indifference, and lack of reverence toward the Blessed Sacrament. Mother, help us to adore Him as you adored Him, with a pure heart and unwavering love.

Reparation Offering: We offer this decade for the renewal of faith and love for Jesus in the Holy Eucharist.

The Sorrowful Mysteries

The Agony in the Garden

Jesus suffers alone, while His disciples sleep. We offer reparation for indifference to His sufferings and the neglect of prayer. *(Matthew 26:36–46)*

Mary, though you were not physically present in Gethsemane, your heart kept vigil with your Son in His loneliness. You shared in His sorrow as He accepted the bitter chalice for our salvation. We offer reparation for all indifference to His agony, for sins of ingratitude, and for every betrayal of His love.

Reparation Offering: We offer this decade for those who are lukewarm in faith and for all who abandon Christ in times of trial.

The Scourging at the Pillar

Jesus is brutally whipped. We make reparation for sins of impurity and for violence against the human body. *(John 19:1)*

Mary, your soul was pierced as you imagined the cruel lashes tearing at your Son's flesh. He endured this torment in reparation for the sins of the flesh and all impurity. We offer reparation for the spread of immorality, for those enslaved by vice, and for the corruption of innocence.

Reparation Offering: We offer this decade for the conversion of those trapped in sins of impurity and for the restoration of purity in hearts and homes.

The Crowning with Thorns

Christ is mocked as King. We offer reparation for blasphemy and the rejection of His kingship. *(Matthew 27:27–31)*

Mary, your heart bled as you envisioned the soldiers mocking your Son, pressing the cruel crown into His sacred head. He bore the wounds for our pride and arrogance. We offer reparation for the rejection of Christ's Kingship, for the sins of vanity, and for the desecration of His holy name.

Reparation Offering: We offer this decade for humility in ourselves and for all to acknowledge Jesus as King.

The Carrying of the Cross

Jesus embraces His Cross for love of us. We make reparation for refusal to accept the crosses God sends. *(Luke 23:26–32)*

Mary, you met your Son on the road to Calvary, sharing His suffering as He bore the weight of the world's sins. We offer reparation for the rejection of the Cross, for the refusal to embrace suffering as a means of sanctification, and for all who rebel against God's will.

Reparation Offering: We offer this decade for those burdened with heavy crosses, that they may unite their suffering with Christ.

The Crucifixion

Mary stands at the foot of the Cross. We unite our hearts with hers in reparation for every sin that pierces the Heart of Christ. *(John 19:25–30)*

Mary, you stood faithfully at the foot of the Cross, your heart pierced with sorrow as you offered your Son to the Father for the salvation of the world. We offer reparation for every sin that nailed Him to the Cross, for blasphemy, and for the desecration of the Lord's Day.

Reparation Offering: We offer this decade for the conversion of sinners and the triumph of Christ's mercy.

The Glorious Mysteries

The Resurrection

Christ rises victorious over sin and death. We make reparation for despair and loss of hope in God's promises. *(Luke 24:1–12)*

Mary, your sorrow was turned to joy when your Son rose in triumph over death. We offer reparation for the denial of the Resurrection, for disbelief in the Gospel, and for all who live without hope in eternal life.

Reparation Offering: We offer this decade for those struggling with despair and for all who have lost the light of faith.

The Ascension

Jesus returns to the Father, promising the Spirit. We offer reparation for neglect of eternal life in favor of worldly gain. *(Acts 1:6–11)*

Mary, you watched with loving faith as your Son returned to the Father, opening Heaven's gates for the redeemed. We offer reparation for those who reject Christ's authority and refuse to follow His commandments.

Reparation Offering: We offer this decade for obedience to God's law and for perseverance in the path that leads to Heaven.

The Descent of the Holy Spirit

The Church is filled with divine fire. We make reparation for resistance to the Holy Spirit's inspirations. *(Acts 2:1–13)*

Mary, you prayed with the Apostles in the Upper Room as the Holy Spirit descended, igniting the Church with divine fire. We offer reparation for the rejection of the Holy Spirit's inspirations and for the sin of indifference to His gifts.

Reparation Offering: We offer this decade for a renewal of faith in the Church and for the courage to bear witness to the Gospel.

The Assumption of Mary

Mary is taken body and soul into heaven. We offer reparation for the denial of her role in salvation history. *(Revelation 12:1)*

Mary, you were taken body and soul into Heaven, the reward of your immaculate purity and faithful love. We offer reparation for the denial of your privileges and for all offences against your Immaculate Heart.

Reparation Offering: We offer this decade for an increase in Marian devotion and for all to turn to you as Mother and Queen.

The Coronation of Mary

Mary is crowned Queen of Heaven and Earth. We make reparation for ingratitude toward her maternal intercession. *(Revelation 12:1–6)*

Mary, you were crowned Queen in the presence of the angels and saints, reigning beside your Son. We offer reparation for the refusal to honor you, for neglect of your maternal intercession, and for all who scorn the heavenly glory prepared for the faithful.

Reparation Offering: We offer this decade for the triumph of your Immaculate Heart and the coming of Christ's reign of peace.

MARIAN ROSARY OF REPARATION (Version 2)

Historical Introduction

The Rosary is not only a crown of roses offered to Our Blessed Mother, but also a powerful weapon of reparation in the hands of the faithful.

When prayed with love and faith, each bead becomes an act of consolation for the wounds of Christ and an offering of comfort to His Mother, who stood faithfully at the foot of the Cross.

In this Marian mission of reparation, the Rosary takes on a deeper dimension: every decade is offered not only in thanksgiving for the mysteries of our salvation, but also in reparation for the sins committed against the Sacred Face of Jesus and the Immaculate Heart of Mary.

As St. Louis de Montfort reminds us, "When we say the Rosary well, we bind a crown of roses for Jesus and Mary."

In the spirit of St. Thérèse of the Child Jesus and the Holy Face, let us approach this prayer as children approaching their Mother, confident that every "Hail Mary" brings joy to her heart and relief to the Heart of her Son.

Rosary of the Blessed Virgin Mary in Reparation

(Joyful Mysteries)

Opening Prayer:

O Most Holy Virgin Mary, Mother of Sorrows and Queen of Martyrs, we unite ourselves to you at the foot of the Cross, offering this Rosary in reparation for the sins committed against your Immaculate Heart and the Sacred Face of your Divine Son. Obtain for us purity of heart, steadfast faith, and courage to bear our daily crosses in union with yours. Amen.

First Joyful Mystery – The Annunciation

We meditate on the moment when the Archangel Gabriel announced to you, O Mary, that you were chosen to be the Mother of God. Your humble "Fiat" opened the way for the Word to become flesh and dwell among us.

Reparation Intention: We offer this decade in reparation for all sins of pride and self-will that oppose the will of God in our lives and in the world.

Grace to Seek: Humility and perfect surrender to God's will.

Second Joyful Mystery – The Visitation

We meditate on your charity in going with haste to help your cousin Elizabeth. You brought with you the hidden Christ, causing John to leap in her womb.

Reparation Intention: We offer this decade in reparation for indifference to the needs of others and for failures to recognize Christ in our neighbor.

Grace to Seek: True charity and zeal to bring Christ to others.

Third Joyful Mystery – The Nativity

We meditate on the birth of Our Lord Jesus Christ in Bethlehem. In poverty and simplicity, you and St. Joseph welcomed the Saviour of the world.

Reparation Intention: We offer this decade in reparation for all irreverence toward the mystery of the Incarnation and for neglect of the poor and vulnerable.

Grace to Seek: A spirit of poverty and detachment from worldly goods.

Fourth Joyful Mystery – The Presentation in the Temple

We meditate on the day you and St. Joseph presented Jesus in the Temple, offering Him to the Father in obedience to the Law. Simeon prophesied that a sword would pierce your soul.

Reparation Intention: We offer this decade in reparation for disobedience to God's law and for the sins of sacrilege.

Grace to Seek: Obedience, purity of heart, and acceptance of God's will.

Fifth Joyful Mystery – The Finding of the Child Jesus in the Temple

We meditate on the sorrow you felt when Jesus was lost for three days, and the joy at finding Him in the Temple, about His Father's business.

Reparation Intention: We offer this decade in reparation for neglect of prayer, catechesis, and devotion in Christian families.

Grace to Seek: Fidelity in seeking Jesus and joy in finding Him in the sacraments.

Closing Prayer:
O Mary, Mother of the Church and Refuge of Sinners, accept these prayers offered in union with your own immaculate and sorrowful heart. Obtain for us the grace to console your Son, to repair for sin, and to live in the peace of His Kingdom. Amen.

Rosary of the Blessed Virgin Mary in Reparation

(Sorrowful Mysteries)

Opening Prayer:

O Mary, Mother most sorrowful, we keep watch with you at the foot of the Cross. We offer this Rosary in reparation for the sins that pierce your Immaculate Heart and disfigure the Holy Face of your Son. Obtain for us true contrition, perseverance in trial, and union with Jesus in His Passion. Amen.

First Sorrowful Mystery – The Agony in the Garden

We meditate on Our Lord's agony in Gethsemane as He accepts the chalice of suffering for our salvation. You, O Mary, interiorly shared in His sorrow, offering your fiat anew.

Reparation Intention: We offer this decade in reparation for all sins of ingratitude, indifference, and refusal to accept the will of God.

Grace to Seek: Courage to accept and unite our sufferings with those of Christ.

Second Sorrowful Mystery – The Scourging at the Pillar

We meditate on the cruel scourging of Jesus, which tore His sacred flesh. You, O Mary, suffered mystically every blow that fell upon Him.

Reparation Intention: We offer this decade in reparation for sins of impurity and the desecration of the human body, temple of the Holy Spirit.

Grace to Seek: Purity of heart, mind, and body.

Third Sorrowful Mystery – The Crowning with Thorns

We meditate on the cruel crowning of Jesus with thorns and the mockery of His kingship. Your heart, O Mary, bled with His as you beheld His Sacred Head so wounded.

Reparation Intention: We offer this decade in reparation for sins of pride, mockery of truth, and rejection of Christ's kingship.

Grace to Seek: Humility and a love for the truth of the Gospel.

Fourth Sorrowful Mystery – The Carrying of the Cross

We meditate on Jesus carrying His Cross to Calvary. You, O Mary, walked beside Him, sharing His burden in your heart.

Reparation Intention: We offer this decade in reparation for those who reject or abandon their crosses, and for the sin of despair.

Grace to Seek: Perseverance and love in carrying our daily crosses.

Fifth Sorrowful Mystery – The Crucifixion and Death of Our Lord

We meditate on the crucifixion of Jesus and your presence at the foot of the Cross, O Mary, uniting yourself fully to His sacrifice.

Reparation Intention: We offer this decade in reparation for all mortal sins, sacrileges, and indifference to the Precious Blood shed for our redemption.

Grace to Seek: Final perseverance, love of the Cross, and trust in Jesus at the hour of death.

Closing Prayer:

O Mary, Queen of Martyrs, accept these prayers offered in reparation and love. Obtain for us the grace to remain faithful beneath the Cross, to comfort your Son, and to share in His victory over sin and death. Amen.

Rosary of the Blessed Virgin Mary in Reparation

(Glorious Mysteries)

Opening Prayer:

O Mary, Queen of Heaven and Mother of the Church, we rejoice with you in the glory of your Son's victory over sin and death. We offer this Rosary in reparation for sins against the Holy Face of Jesus and your Immaculate Heart, and in thanksgiving for the triumph of grace. Amen.

First Glorious Mystery – The Resurrection

We meditate on the glorious Resurrection of Jesus, when death was conquered forever. O Mary, your sorrow was turned to joy as you beheld your risen Son.

Reparation Intention: We offer this decade in reparation for the sin of unbelief and denial of Christ's divinity.

Grace to Seek: Living faith in the Risen Lord and a spirit of hope.

Second Glorious Mystery – The Ascension

We meditate on the Ascension of Jesus into heaven, where He prepares a place for us. O Mary, you gazed upward with longing, your heart united to His.

Reparation Intention: We offer this decade in reparation for neglect of the eternal truths and the loss of desire for heaven.

Grace to Seek: A deeper longing for union with God in heaven.

Third Glorious Mystery – The Descent of the Holy Spirit

We meditate on the coming of the Holy Spirit upon Mary and the Apostles in the Upper Room. You, O Mary, were the perfect Spouse of the Holy Spirit, interceding for the newborn Church.

Reparation Intention: We offer this decade in reparation for resistance to the inspirations of the Holy Spirit and the rejection of His gifts.

Grace to Seek: Docility to the Holy Spirit and zeal for souls.

Fourth Glorious Mystery – The Assumption of Our Lady into Heaven

We meditate on the Assumption of Mary into heaven, body and soul, where you were crowned with glory.

Reparation Intention: We offer this decade in reparation for the refusal to honor you, O Mary, as Mother and Queen.

Grace to Seek: Greater devotion to Our Lady and trust in her intercession.

Fifth Glorious Mystery– The Coronation of Our Lady as Queen of Heaven and Earth

We meditate on Mary's coronation as Queen of Heaven and Earth, sharing forever in her Son's glory.

Reparation Intention: We offer this decade in reparation for those who reject your maternal love and the reign of Christ the King.

Grace to Seek: Perseverance in grace and final union with God in heaven.

Closing Prayer:

O Mary, Queen of Heaven, accept these prayers offered in reparation and love. May your Immaculate Heart reign in every soul, leading us to the eternal triumph of your Son. Amen.

Meditation on the Seven Sorrows of Mary

*(Short format, suitable for inclusion
in a Holy Hour or private devotion.)*

1. The Prophecy of Simeon

2. The Flight into Egypt

3. The Loss of the Child Jesus in the Temple

4. The Meeting of Jesus and Mary on the Way
    to Calvary

5. The Crucifixion and Death of Jesus

6. The Body of Jesus is Placed in the Arms of
    His Mother

7. The Burial of Jesus

Conclude with:

"Mary, full of sorrows, Mother of the Crucified, teach us
to stand faithfully at the foot of the Cross, offering
ourselves with You for the salvation of souls."

Chaplet of the Seven Sorrows of Mary

(For Reparation and Union with the
Sufferings of the Mother of God)

The Chaplet of the Seven Sorrows is prayed to meditate on the profound sufferings Our Blessed Mother endured during the Passion of Our Lord, and to unite ourselves to her in making reparation for sin.

Opening Prayer

O Most Sorrowful and Immaculate Heart of Mary, I unite myself to your tears, your anguish, and your unfailing love.

Obtain for me the grace to truly repent of my sins and to console the Heart of your Divine Son.

Amen.

First Sorrow: The Prophecy of Simeon

Scripture:

"Simeon blessed them and said to Mary his mother, 'Behold, this child is destined for the fall and rise of many in Israel, and to be a sign that will be contradicted — and a sword will pierce your own soul — that the thoughts of many hearts may be revealed.'" (Luke 2:34–35)

Meditation:

Mary, holding her newborn Child in the Temple, hears the aged Simeon foretell the suffering and rejection that Jesus will endure — and the piercing sorrow that will wound her own soul. Even in the joy of presenting Him to God, she accepts the shadow of the Cross.

Prayer:

Most Sorrowful Mother, obtain for me the grace to accept the sufferings that come into my life with faith and trust.

Pray: 1 Our Father and 7 Hail Marys.

Second Sorrow: The Flight into Egypt

Scripture:

"Joseph rose and took the child and his mother by night and departed for Egypt. He stayed there until the death of Herod, so that what the Lord had said through the prophet might be fulfilled: 'Out of Egypt I called my son.'"(Matthew 2:14–15)

Meditation:

Fleeing in haste under the cover of night, Mary and Joseph protect the Infant Jesus from the murderous rage of Herod. The cold, the fear, and the uncertainty of exile pierce Mary's heart as she carries the Light of the World into a foreign land.

Prayer:

Mother of Refugees, teach me to trust God's providence in the midst of danger and loss.

Pray: 1 Our Father and 7 Hail Marys.

Third Sorrow: The Loss of the Child Jesus in the Temple

Scripture:

"After three days they found him in the temple, sitting among the teachers, listening to them and asking them questions; and all who heard him were astounded at his understanding and his answers." (Luke 2:46–47)

Meditation:

For three long days, Mary and Joseph search in anguish for their beloved Son, not knowing where He is or what has happened to Him. The joy of finding Him in the Temple is mingled with awe at His words and mission.

Prayer:

O Mother who sought the Lost Child, intercede for all who are far from God, that they may return to the Father's house.

Pray: 1 Our Father and 7 Hail Marys.

Fourth Sorrow: Mary Meets
Jesus on the Road to Calvary

Scripture:

"As they led him away, they seized Simon of Cyrene, who was coming from the country, and laid the cross on him to carry behind Jesus. A large crowd of people followed him, including women who mourned and lamented him." (Luke 23:26–27)

Meditation:

Amid the jeers of the crowd and the soldiers' cruelty, Mary meets her Son, bloodied and exhausted. Their eyes meet in silent understanding—two hearts united in the same sacrifice for the salvation of the world.

Prayer:

O Mother of Sorrows, help me to carry my cross with patience and love, and to see Jesus in all who suffer.

Pray: 1 Our Father and 7 Hail Marys.

Fifth Sorrow: The Crucifixion and Death of Jesus

Scripture:

"Standing by the cross of Jesus were his mother and his mother's sister, Mary the wife of Clopas, and Mary Magdalene. When Jesus saw his mother and the disciple there whom he loved, he said to his mother, 'Woman, behold, your son.' Then he said to the disciple, 'Behold, your mother.' And from that hour the disciple took her into his home."

(John 19:25–27)

Meditation:

Mary stands at the foot of the Cross, watching her Son's agony, hearing His final words, and receiving the beloved disciple — and all of us — into her care.

Prayer:

O Mother, teach me to stand firm in faith at the foot of every cross, trusting in the victory of your Son.

Pray: 1 Our Father and 7 Hail Marys.

Sixth Sorrow: Mary Receives the Body of Jesus

Scripture:

"Joseph of Arimathea came and took his body down. He wrapped it in linen and laid him in a tomb cut in the rock, where no one had ever been laid." (Luke 23:53)

Meditation:

Mary receives the lifeless Body of her Son, cradling Him as she did in Bethlehem, but now broken, cold, and pierced for our sins. Her grief is deep, yet her trust in God's plan is unshaken.

Prayer:

O Mother most faithful, help me to embrace the will of God even when it is mysterious and painful.

Pray: 1 Our Father and 7 Hail Marys.

Seventh Sorrow: The Burial of Jesus

Scripture:

"They rolled a great stone against the entrance of the tomb and went away. Mary Magdalene and the other Mary remained sitting there, facing the tomb."

(Matthew 27:60–61)

Meditation:

Mary watches as the tomb is sealed, entrusting her Son to the Father's promise. The silence of Holy Saturday begins—a time of waiting, faith, and hope in the Resurrection.

Prayer:

O Mother of Hope, teach me to trust in God's power to bring life from death.

Pray: 1 Our Father and 7 Hail Marys.

Closing Prayer

O Mother of Sorrows, by the merits of your tears and your faithful suffering, obtain for us the grace of a holy death and the joy of eternal life with Jesus. Amen.

The Little
Chaplet
of the Holy Face

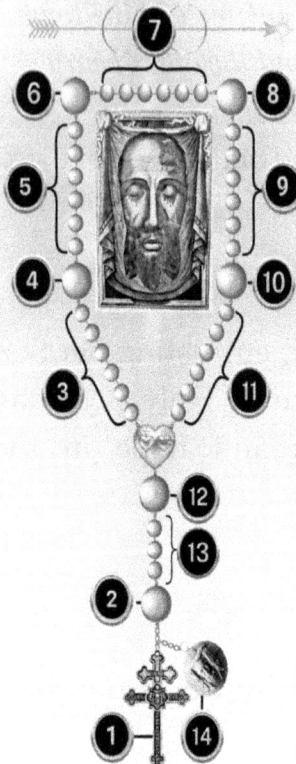

1

On the Crucifix make the sign of the Cross.
O God, come to my assistance; O Lord make haste to help me.
Glory be to the Father and to the Son and to the Holy Ghost. As it was in the beginning, is now, and ever shall be, world without end. Amen.

2

My Jesus, Mercy. In honour of the sense of Touch.

Glory be to the Father and to the Son and to the Holy Ghost. As it was in the beginning, is now, and ever shall be, world without end. Amen.

3

Arise, O Lord, and let Thine enemies be scattered, and let them that hate Thee flee from before Thy Face. (X6)

4

My Jesus, Mercy. In honour of the sense of Hearing.

Glory be to the Father and to the Son and to the Holy Ghost. As it was in the beginning, is now, and ever shall be, world without end. Amen.

5

Arise, O Lord, and let Thine enemies be scattered, and let them that hate Thee flee from before Thy Face. (X6)

6

My Jesus, Mercy. In honour of the sense of Sight.

Glory be to the Father and to the Son and to the Holy Ghost. As it was in the beginning, is now, and ever shall be, world without end. Amen.

7

Arise, O Lord, and let Thine enemies be scattered, and let them that hate Thee flee from before Thy Face. (X6)

8

My Jesus, Mercy. In honour of the sense of Smell.

Glory be to the Father and to the Son and to the Holy Ghost. As it was in the beginning, is now, and ever shall be, world without end. Amen.

9

Arise, O Lord, and let Thine enemies be scattered, and let them that hate Thee flee from before Thy Face. (X6)

10

My Jesus, Mercy. In honour of the sense of Taste.

Glory be to the Father and to the Son and to the Holy Ghost. As it was in the beginning, is now, and ever shall be, world without end. Amen.

11

Arise, O Lord, and let Thine enemies be scattered, and let them that hate Thee flee from before Thy Face. (X6)

12

My Jesus, Mercy. Let us recall to mind the public life of the Saviour and let us honour all the wounds of His adorable Face.

Glory be to the Father and to the Son and to the Holy Ghost. As it was in the beginning, is now, and ever shall be, world without end. Amen.

13

Arise, O Lord, and let Thine enemies be scattered, and let them that hate Thee flee from before Thy Face. (X3)

14

On the Holy Face Medal pray: God, our Protector, look on us, and cast Thy eyes upon the Face of Thy Christ. Amen.

On the Crucifix make the sign of the Cross.

ADDITIONAL PRAYERS

ETERNAL FATHER, I offer Thee the Cross of our Lord Jesus Christ and all the other instruments of His Holy Passion, that Thou mayst put division in the camp of Thine enemies, as Thy beloved Son has said: "A kingdom divided against itself shall fall".

May the thrice Holy Name of God overthrow all their plans.

May the Name of the Living God split them up by disagreements.

May the terrible Name of the God of Eternity stamp out all their godlessness!

O Lord, I desire not the death of the sinner, but that he be converted and live: "Father, forgive them for they know not what they do."

Nihil Obstat: Fr. Thomas Hoisington, S.T.L.
Censor Librorum April 11, 2025

Imprimatur: ✠ Bishop Carl A. Kemme
Bishop of Wichita April 11, 2025

The Little Chaplet of the Holy Face

The little chaplet of the Holy Face is to be prayed using a special chaplet of beads that consists of thirty-three beads made up of five sets of six beads, and one set containing three beads. The first five sets are prayed to make reparation for the many sins and offences against Our Blessed Lord's Holy Face experienced through His five senses of touch, hearing, sight, smell and taste. The remaining set of three beads are prayed in honor of the three years of our Blessed Lord's public ministry on earth.

A diagram has been included in this chapter for instructional purposes.

1. On the Crucifix, make the Sign of the Cross and *Pray:* O God, come to my assistance; O Lord, make haste to help me. Glory be to the Father, and to the Son, and to the Holy Ghost. As it was in the beginning, is now, and ever shall be, world without end. Amen.

2. *Pray:* My Jesus Mercy. **In Honor of the Sense of Touch**. Glory be to the Father, and to the Son, and to the Holy Ghost. As it was in the beginning, is now, and ever shall be, world without end. Amen.

3. *Invocation:*

Arise, O Lord, and let Thine enemies be scattered, and let them that hate Thee flee from before Thy Face. (×6)

4. *Pray:* My Jesus Mercy. **In Honor of the Sense of Hearing**. Glory be to the Father, and to the Son, and to the Holy Ghost. As it was in the beginning, is now, and ever shall be, world without end. Amen.

5. *Invocation:*

Arise, O Lord, and let Thine enemies be scattered, and let them that hate Thee flee from before Thy Face. (×6)

6. *Pray:* My Jesus Mercy. **In Honor of the Sense of Sight.** Glory be to the Father, and to the Son, and to the Holy Ghost. As it was in the beginning, is now, and ever shall be, world without end. Amen.

7. *Invocation:*

Arise, O Lord, and let Thine enemies be scattered, and let them that hate Thee flee from before Thy Face. (×6)

8. *Pray:* My Jesus Mercy. **In Honor of the Sense of Smell.** Glory be to the Father, and to the Son, and to the Holy Ghost. As it was in the beginning, is now, and ever shall be, world without end. Amen.

9. *Invocation:*

Arise, O Lord, and let Thine enemies be scattered, and let them that hate Thee flee from before Thy Face. (×6)

10. *Pray:* My Jesus Mercy. **In Honor of the Sense of Taste.** Glory be to the Father, and to the Son, and to the Holy Ghost. As it was in the beginning, is now, and ever shall be, world without end. Amen.

11. *Invocation*:

Arise, O Lord, and let Thine enemies be scattered, and let them that hate Thee flee from before Thy Face. (×6)

12. *Pray:* My Jesus Mercy. **Let Us Recall the Public Life of the Saviour, and let us honor all the wounds of His adorable Face.** Glory be to the Father, and to the Son, and to the Holy Ghost. As it was in the beginning, is now, and ever shall be, world without end. Amen.

13. *Invocation:*

Arise, O Lord, and let Thine enemies be scattered, and let them that hate Thee flee from before Thy Face. (×3)

14. *Pray:* On the Holy Face Medal, pray:

God, our Protector, look on us, and cast Thy eyes upon the Face of Thy Christ. Amen.

Most beautiful Face of Jesus, so full of pity and sweetness, turn towards us Thy merciful gaze, and have compassion on us. May we never turn our eyes away from Thee but seek Thee in all creatures. May Thy image be ever imprinted in our hearts. Amen.

Prayer of St. Thérèse of the Child Jesus and the Holy Face

O Jesus, who in Your cruel Passion became "the reproach of men and the Man of sorrows," I venerate Your divine Face, upon which shone the beauty and gentleness of the Divinity, but which became for my sake the face of a "leper."

In those disfigured features, I recognize Your infinite love, and I long to love You and make You loved. I implore You to imprint Your divine likeness upon me, and to inflame me with Your love, that I may be able to contemplate Your glorious Face in heaven.
Amen.

Closing Marian Act of Reparation

O Mary, Mother of the Crucified,
I offer You the sufferings of Your Son's adorable Face,
united with the sorrows of Your Immaculate Heart,
in reparation for every blasphemy,
every profanation of the Most Holy Eucharist,
and every wound inflicted upon Holy Mother Church.
Through Your intercession,
may sinners be converted,
the lukewarm set aflame,
and the faithful made strong in the face of trial. Amen.

Consecration to the Holy Face

I ...., in order to give still greater increase to the glory of Jesus, dying for our salvation upon the Cross; in order to correspond to the merciful love with which His Holy Face is animated towards poor sinners, and in order to repair the outrages which the frightful crimes of the present day inflict upon His august Face, the most pure mirror of the divine Majesty, I associate myself, fully and freely, to the faithful received into this pious confraternity; I desire to participate in the indulgences with which it is enriched and in the good works practiced therein, as well for the expiation of my sins as for the solace of souls suffering in Purgatory.

Amiable Redeemer, most sweet Jesus, hide in the secret of Thy Face all the members of this association; may they there find shelter from the seductions of the world, and the snares of Satan; grant that, faithfully keeping all the precepts of Thy law and fulfilling the special duties of their state, they may be more and more inflamed with zeal for reparation, and with the flames of Thy divine love.

Appendix II:
Litanies of Our Lady

LITANY OF LORETO

Lord, have mercy on us.
Christ, have mercy on us.
Lord, have mercy on us.
Christ, hear us.
Christ, graciously hear us.
God the Father of Heaven, *have mercy on us.*
God the Son, Redeemer of the world, *have mercy on us.*
God the Holy Spirit, *have mercy on us.*
Holy Trinity, One God, *have mercy on us.*
Holy Mary, *pray for us.*
Holy Mother of God, *pray for us.*
Holy Virgin of virgins, *pray for us.*
Mother of Christ, *pray for us.*
Mother of the Church, *pray for us.*
Mother of divine grace, *pray for us.*
Mother most pure, *pray for us.*
Mother most chaste, *pray for us.*
Mother inviolate, *pray for us.*
Mother undefiled, *pray for us.*
Mother most amiable, *pray for us.*
Mother most admirable, *pray for us.*

Mother of good counsel, *pray for us.*
Mother of our Creator, *pray for us.*
Mother of our Saviour, *pray for us.*
Virgin most prudent, *pray for us.*
Virgin most venerable, *pray for us.*
Virgin most renowned, *pray for us.*
Virgin most powerful, *pray for us.*
Virgin most merciful, *pray for us.*
Virgin most faithful, *pray for us.*
Mirror of justice, *pray for us.*
Seat of wisdom, *pray for us.*
Cause of our joy, *pray for us.*
Spiritual vessel, *pray for us.*
Vessel of honor, *pray for us.*
Singular vessel of devotion, *pray for us.*
Mystical rose, *pray for us.*
Tower of David, *pray for us.*
Tower of ivory, *pray for us.*
House of gold, *pray for us.*
Ark of the covenant, *pray for us.*
Gate of Heaven, *pray for us.*
Morning star, *pray for us.*
Health of the sick, *pray for us.*
Refuge of sinners, *pray for us.*
Comforter of the afflicted, *pray for us.*
Help of Christians, *pray for us.*
Queen of angels, *pray for us.*
Queen of patriarchs, *pray for us.*

Queen of prophets, *pray for us.*
Queen of apostles, *pray for us.*
Queen of martyrs, *pray for us.*
Queen of confessors, *pray for us.*
Queen of virgins, *pray for us.*
Queen of all saints, *pray for us.*
Queen conceived without original sin, *pray for us.*
Queen assumed into Heaven, *pray for us.*
Queen of the Most Holy Rosary, *pray for us.*
Queen of families, *pray for us.*
Queen of peace, *pray for us.*
Lamb of God, who takest away the sins of the world,
spare us, O Lord.
Lamb of God, who takest away the sins of the world,
graciously hear us, O Lord.
Lamb of God, who takest away the sins of the world,
have mercy on us.

V. Pray for us, O holy Mother of God.
R. *That we may be made worthy of the promises of Christ.*

Let us pray.
Grant, we beseech Thee, O Lord God, that we, Thy servants, may enjoy perpetual health of mind and body; and by the glorious intercession of Blessed Mary ever Virgin, may we be delivered from present sorrow and obtain eternal joy. Through Christ our Lord.
Amen.

LITANY OF OUR LADY OF THE HOLY FACE

*(Composed in honor of Mary's role in the
devotion to the Holy Face of Jesus)*

Lord, have mercy on us.
Christ, have mercy on us.
Lord, have mercy on us.
Christ, hear us.
Christ, graciously hear us.
God the Father of Heaven, *have mercy on us.*
God the Son, Redeemer of the world, *have mercy on us.*
God the Holy Spirit, *have mercy on us.*
Holy Trinity, One God, *have mercy on us.*
Holy Mary, *pray for us.*
Our Lady of the Holy Face, *pray for us.*
Our Lady, in whose pure countenance the light of
Christ shines, *pray for us.*
Our Lady, mirror of the Face of Christ, *pray for us.*
Our Lady, who reflected the beauty of your Son's
holiness, *pray for us.*
Our Lady, whose soul magnified the Lord, *pray for us.*
Our Lady, who treasured all things in your heart, *pray
for us.*
Our Lady, whose eyes beheld the Face of the Infant
Jesus, *pray for us.*
Our Lady, who consoled the Face of Christ in His
Passion, *pray for us.*

Our Lady, who wiped away His sacred tears, *pray for us.*
Our Lady, who stood beside the Cross gazing on the
Face of the Crucified, *pray for us.*
Our Lady, who received the lifeless Body of Jesus in
your arms, *pray for us.*
Our Lady, who saw the light of Easter in His risen Face,
pray for us.
Our Lady, whose prayers draw us to contemplate His
Holy Face, *pray for us.*
Vessel of the Incarnation, *pray for us.*
Comfort of the sorrowful, *pray for us.*
Help of the afflicted, *pray for us.*
Mother of perpetual help, *pray for us.*
Queen of the Rosary, *pray for us.*
Queen of martyrs, *pray for us.*
Queen of peace, *pray for us.*
Lamb of God, who takest away the sins of the world,
spare us, O Lord.
Lamb of God, who takest away the sins of the world,
graciously hear us, O Lord.
Lamb of God, who takest away the sins of the world,
have mercy on us.

V. Pray for us, O holy Mother of God.
R. *That we may be made worthy of the promises of Christ.*

Let us pray.

O Mary, our Lady of the Holy Face, by your loving contemplation of the Face of Jesus, draw us ever closer to your Son. May we, through your intercession, console Him for the outrages He has suffered and offer our lives in reparation to His Sacred Face. Through the same Christ our Lord. *Amen.*

LITANY OF THE IMMACULATE HEART OF MARY

Lord, have mercy on us.
Christ, have mercy on us.
Lord, have mercy on us.
Christ, hear us.
Christ, graciously hear us.
God the Father of Heaven, *have mercy on us.*
God the Son, Redeemer of the world, *have mercy on us.*
God the Holy Spirit, *have mercy on us.*
Holy Trinity, One God, *have mercy on us.*
Heart of Mary, immaculate from the first moment of your conception, *pray for us.*
Heart of Mary, full of grace, *pray for us.*
Heart of Mary, blessed among all hearts, *pray for us.*
Heart of Mary, throne of glory, *pray for us.*
Heart of Mary, most humble, *pray for us.*

Heart of Mary, holocaust of Divine Love, *pray for us.*
Heart of Mary, fastened to the Cross with Jesus
Crucified, *pray for us.*
Heart of Mary, comfort of the afflicted, *pray for us.*
Heart of Mary, refuge of sinners, *pray for us.*
Heart of Mary, hope of the agonizing, *pray for us.*
Heart of Mary, seat of mercy, *pray for us.*
Lamb of God, who takest away the sins of the world,
spare us, O Lord.
Lamb of God, who takest away the sins of the world,
graciously hear us, O Lord.
Lamb of God, who takest away the sins of the world,
have mercy on us.

V. Pray for us, O holy Mother of God.
R. *That we may be made worthy of the promises of Christ.*

Let us pray.

O most merciful God, who for the salvation of sinners
and the refuge of the wretched has made the
Immaculate Heart of Mary most like in charity and
mercy to the Heart of Jesus, grant that we, who now
commemorate her most sweet and loving Heart, may by
her merits and intercession ever live in the fellowship of
the Hearts of both Mother and Son. Through the same
Christ our Lord. *Amen.*

LITANY OF OUR LADY OF SORROWS

Lord, have mercy on us.
Christ, have mercy on us.
Lord, have mercy on us. Christ, hear us.
Christ, graciously hear us.

God the Father of Heaven, *have mercy on us.*
God the Son, Redeemer of the world, *have mercy on us.*
God the Holy Spirit, *have mercy on us.*
Holy Trinity, One God, *have mercy on us.*

Holy Mary, *pray for us.*
Holy Mother of God, *pray for us.*
Holy Virgin of virgins, *pray for us.*

Mother crucified, *pray for us.*
Mother sorrowful, *pray for us.*
Mother tearful, *pray for us.*
Mother afflicted, *pray for us.*
Mother forsaken, *pray for us.*
Mother desolate, *pray for us.*
Mother bereft of your Son, *pray for us.*

Virgin obedient, *pray for us.*
Virgin faithful, *pray for us.*
Virgin of compassion, *pray for us.*
Virgin most sorrowful, *pray for us.*

Fountain of tears, *pray for us.*
Sea of bitterness, *pray for us.*
Field of tribulation, *pray for us.*
Mass of suffering, *pray for us.*
Mirror of patience, *pray for us.*
Rock of constancy, *pray for us.*
Anchor in grief, *pray for us.*
Refuge of the forsaken, *pray for us.*

Shield of the oppressed, *pray for us.*
Subduer of the unbelieving, *pray for us.*
Comfort of the afflicted, *pray for us.*
Medicine of the sick, *pray for us.*
Help of the faint, *pray for us.*
Strength of the weak, *pray for us.*

Protectress of those who fight, *pray for us.*
Haven of the shipwrecked, *pray for us.*
Calmer of tempests, *pray for us.*
Companion of the sorrowful, *pray for us.*
Retreat of those who groan, *pray for us.*
Terror of the treacherous, *pray for us.*

Standard-bearer of the Martyrs, *pray for us.*
Treasure of the Faithful, *pray for us.*
Light of Confessors, *pray for us.*
Pearl of Virgins, *pray for us.*

Comfort of Widows, *pray for us.*
Joy of all Saints, *pray for us.*

Lamb of God, who takest away the sins of the world, *spare us, O Lord.*
Lamb of God, who takest away the sins of the world, *graciously hear us, O Lord.*
Lamb of God, who takest away the sins of the world, *have mercy on us.*

V. Pray for us, most sorrowful Virgin.
R. That we may be made worthy of the promises of Christ.

Let us pray.

Let intercession be made for us, we beseech You, O Lord Jesus Christ, now and at the hour of our death, before the throne of Your mercy, by the Blessed Virgin Mary, Your Mother, whose most holy soul was pierced by a sword of sorrow in the hour of Your bitter Passion. Through You, Jesus Christ, Saviour of the world, who with the Father and the Holy Spirit lives and reigns world without end. *Amen.*

LITANY OF THE BLESSED VIRGIN MARY FOR REPARATION

Lord, have mercy on us.
Christ, have mercy on us.
Lord, have mercy on us. Christ, hear us.
Christ, graciously hear us.
God the Father of Heaven, *have mercy on us.*
God the Son, Redeemer of the world, *have mercy on us.*
God the Holy Spirit, *have mercy on us.*
Holy Trinity, One God, *have mercy on us.*
Holy Mary, *pray for us.*
Holy Mother of God, *pray for us.*
Holy Virgin of virgins, *pray for us.*
Mother of the Church, *pray for us.*
Mother of divine grace, *pray for us.*
Mother most pure, *pray for us.*
Mother most chaste, *pray for us.*
Mother inviolate, *pray for us.*
Mother undefiled, *pray for us.*
Mother most amiable, *pray for us.*
Mother most admirable, *pray for us.*
Mother of good counsel, *pray for us.*
Mother of our Creator, *pray for us.*
Mother of our Saviour, *pray for us.*
Virgin most prudent, *pray for us.*
Virgin most venerable, *pray for us.*
Virgin most renowned, *pray for us.*

Virgin most powerful, *pray for us.*
Virgin most merciful, *pray for us.*
Virgin most faithful, *pray for us.*
Mirror of justice, *pray for us.*
Seat of wisdom, *pray for us.*
Cause of our joy, *pray for us.*
Spiritual vessel, *pray for us.*
Vessel of honor, *pray for us.*
Singular vessel of devotion, *pray for us.*
Mystical rose, *pray for us.*
Tower of David, *pray for us.*
Tower of ivory, *pray for us.*
House of gold, *pray for us.*
Ark of the covenant, *pray for us.*
Gate of Heaven, *pray for us.*
Morning star, *pray for us.*
Health of the sick, *pray for us.*
Refuge of sinners, *pray for us.*
Comforter of the afflicted, *pray for us.*
Help of Christians, *pray for us.*
Queen of Angels, *pray for us.*
Queen of Patriarchs, *pray for us.*
Queen of Prophets, *pray for us.*
Queen of Apostles, *pray for us.*
Queen of Martyrs, *pray for us.*
Queen of Confessors, *pray for us.*
Queen of Virgins, *pray for us.*
Queen of All Saints, *pray for us.*

Queen conceived without Original Sin, *pray for us.*
Queen assumed into Heaven, *pray for us.*
Queen of the Most Holy Rosary, *pray for us.*
Queen of Peace, *pray for us.*
Lamb of God, who takest away the sins of the world, *spare us, O Lord.*
Lamb of God, who takest away the sins of the world, *graciously hear us, O Lord.*
Lamb of God, who takest away the sins of the world, *have mercy on us.*

V. Pray for us, O Holy Mother of God.
R. That we may be made worthy of the promises of Christ.

Let us pray.

O God, whose only-begotten Son, by His life, death, and resurrection, has purchased for us the rewards of eternal salvation: grant, we beseech You, that meditating on the mysteries of the most holy Rosary of the Blessed Virgin Mary, we may imitate what they contain and obtain what they promise, through the same Christ our Lord. *Amen.*

Appendix III:
Treasury of Marian Prayers

Consecration to Mary (St. Louis de Montfort)

I, _____, a faithless sinner, renew and ratify today in thy hands, O Immaculate Mother, the vows of my Baptism. I renounce forever Satan, his pomps and works, and I give myself entirely to Jesus Christ, the Incarnate Wisdom, to carry my cross after Him all the days of my life, and to be more faithful to Him than I have ever been before.

In the presence of all the heavenly court, I choose thee this day for my Mother and Mistress. I deliver and consecrate to thee, as thy slave, my body and soul, my goods, both interior and exterior, and even the value of all my good actions, past, present and future; leaving to thee the entire and full right of disposing of me, and all that belongs to me, without exception, according to thy good pleasure, for the greater glory of God in time and in eternity. Amen.

Act of Consecration to the Immaculata
(*St. Maximilian Kolbe*)

O Immaculata, Queen of heaven and earth, refuge of sinners and our most loving Mother, God has willed to entrust the entire order of mercy to you.

I, _____, a repentant sinner, cast myself at your feet, humbly imploring you to take me with all that I am and have, wholly to yourself as your possession and property.

Please make of me, of all my powers of soul and body, of my whole life, death, and eternity, whatever most pleases you.

If it pleases you, use all that I am and have without reserve, wholly to accomplish what was said of you: "She will crush your head," and, "You alone have destroyed all heresies in the whole world."

Let me be a fit instrument in your immaculate and most merciful hands for introducing and increasing your glory to the greatest possible number of strayed and indifferent souls and thus help extend as far as possible the blessed kingdom of the most Sacred Heart of Jesus.

For wherever you enter, you obtain the grace of conversion and growth in holiness, since it is through your hands that all graces come to us from the most Sacred Heart of Jesus.

Allow me to praise you, O most holy Virgin. Give me strength against your enemies. Amen.

Short Daily Renewal of Consecration
(recommended by Kolbe for everyday use)

O Mary, conceived without sin,

pray for us who have recourse to you,

and for all who do not have recourse to you —

especially the enemies of the Holy Church

and all those recommended to you.

Immaculata, I am entirely yours,

and all that I have is yours.

Use me as you will

for the glory of God
and the salvation of souls.

Amen.

Act of Consecration to the
Immaculate Heart of Mary (Fatima)

O Mary, Virgin and most powerful Mother of Mercy, Queen of Heaven and Refuge of sinners, we consecrate ourselves today to your Immaculate Heart. We give you our whole being and all that we have, our life, our home, our family. We wish to belong entirely to you, and to do all things with you, through you, and for you.

We renew today the promises of our Baptism and our Confirmation. We undertake to live as good Christians, faithful to God, the Church, and the Holy Father. We desire to pray the Rosary daily, to offer our prayers, sufferings, and sacrifices in reparation for sin, and for the conversion of sinners.

O Immaculate Heart of Mary, we place our trust in you. Lead us ever closer to your Divine Son, Jesus, and protect us always under your mantle. Amen.

Act of Consecration to the
Immaculate Heart of Mary (Short Form)

O Mary, Virgin most powerful and Mother of mercy, Queen of Heaven and Refuge of sinners, we consecrate ourselves to your Immaculate Heart.

We consecrate to you our very being and our whole life; all that we have, all that we love, all that we are.

To you we give our bodies, our hearts, our souls, and our homes.

To you we give our country and our world.
To you we entrust the future of the Church.

Reign over us, dearest Mother, that we may be yours in prosperity and in adversity, in joy and in sorrow, in health and in sickness, in life and in death.

O most compassionate Heart of Mary, Queen of Heaven, watch over our minds and hearts and preserve them from the influence of the evil one. May your pure love embrace us, protect us, and lead us to your Son, our Lord Jesus Christ.

Amen.

Prayer of Reparation to the Immaculate Heart

O Most Holy Virgin and our Mother, we listen with grief to the complaints of your Immaculate Heart surrounded with the thorns which ungrateful men place therein at every moment by their blasphemies and ingratitude. Moved by the ardent desire of loving you as our Mother and of promoting a true devotion to your Immaculate Heart, we prostrate ourselves at your feet to prove the sorrow we feel for the grief that men cause you and to atone, by means of our prayers and sacrifices, for the offences with which men return your love. Amen.

Prayer to Mary at the Foot of the Cross
(Fulton J. Sheen)

Mary, my Mother, you stood at the foot of the Cross of your Son with unshaken faith, sharing in His suffering and accepting your role in the mystery of redemption. Teach me to unite my sufferings with yours and with His for the salvation of souls. Help me to remain faithful in my trials, and to embrace my cross with love and trust in God's will. Amen.

Sub Tuum Praesidium

Latin:

Sub tuum praesidium confugimus, sancta Dei Genitrix; nostras deprecationes ne despicias in necessitatibus nostris, sed a periculis cunctis libera nos semper, Virgo gloriosa et benedicta.

English:

We fly to thy protection, O Holy Mother of God; despise not our petitions in our necessities, but deliver us always from all dangers, O glorious and blessed Virgin.

Memorare

Latin:

Memorare, O piissima Virgo Maria, non esse auditum a saeculo, quemquam ad tua currentem praesidia, tua implorantem auxilia, tua petentem suffragia esse derelictum. Ego tali animatus confidentia, ad te, Virgo Virginum, Mater, curro; ad te venio; coram te gemens peccator assisto. Noli, Mater Verbi, verba mea despicere; sed audi propitia et exaudi. Amen.

English:

Remember, O most gracious Virgin Mary, that never was it known that anyone who fled to thy protection, implored thy help, or sought thy intercession was left unaided. Inspired by this confidence, I fly unto thee, O Virgin of virgins, my Mother; to thee do I come, before thee I stand, sinful and sorrowful. O Mother of the Word Incarnate, despise not my petitions, but in thy mercy hear and answer me. Amen.

Regina Caeli

Latin:

Regina caeli, laetare, alleluia: Quia quem meruisti portare, alleluia, Resurrexit, sicut dixit, alleluia: Ora pro nobis Deum, alleluia.

English:

Queen of Heaven, rejoice, alleluia: For He whom thou didst merit to bear, alleluia, Hath risen as He said, alleluia: Pray for us to God, alleluia.

Salve Regina

Latin:

Salve, Regina, mater misericordiae; vita, dulcedo, et spes nostra, salve. Ad te clamamus exsules filii Hevae. Ad te suspiramus, gementes et flentes in hac lacrimarum valle. Eia ergo, advocata nostra, illos tuos misericordes oculos ad nos converte; et Jesum, benedictum fructum ventris tui, nobis post hoc exsilium ostende. O clemens, O pia, O dulcis Virgo Maria.

English:

Hail, Holy Queen, Mother of mercy; our life, our sweetness, and our hope. To thee do we cry, poor banished children of Eve. To thee do we send up our sighs, mourning and weeping in this valley of tears. Turn then, most gracious advocate, thine eyes of mercy toward us, and after this our exile show unto us the blessed fruit of thy womb, Jesus. O clement, O loving, O sweet Virgin Mary.

Appendix IV:
Devotions and Meditations

The Angelus in Latin

V. Angelus Dómini nuntiávit Maríæ.
R. Et concépit de Spíritu Sancto.
Ave María, grátia plena…

V. Ecce ancílla Dómini.
R. Fiat mihi secúndum verbum tuum.
Ave María, grátia plena…

V. Et Verbum caro factum est.
R. Et habitávit in nobis.
Ave María, grátia plena…

V. Ora pro nobis, sancta Dei Génetrix.
R. Ut digni efficiámur promissiónibus Christi.

Oremus:

Grátiam tuam, quæsumus Dómine, méntibus nostris infúnde: ut qui, Angelo nuntiánte, Christi Fílii tui Incarnatiónem cognóvimus, per passiónem ejus et crucem ad resurrectiónis glóriam perducámur. Per eúndem Christum Dóminum nostrum.
Amen.

The Angelus

V. The Angel of the Lord declared unto Mary.
R. And she conceived of the Holy Spirit.
Hail Mary, full of grace…

V. Behold the handmaid of the Lord.
R. Be it done unto me according to Thy word.
Hail Mary, full of grace…

V. And the Word was made Flesh.
R. And dwelt among us.
Hail Mary, full of grace…

V. Pray for us, O holy Mother of God.
R. That we may be made worthy of the promises of Christ.

Let us pray:

Pour forth, we beseech Thee, O Lord, Thy grace into our hearts; that we, to whom the Incarnation of Christ, Thy Son, was made known by the message of an angel, may by His Passion and Cross be brought to the glory of His Resurrection. Through the same Christ Our Lord. Amen.

Fulton Sheen's Stations of the Cross
(Short Version)

This holy devotion commemorates the various incidents that occurred during Our Lord's painful journey with His Cross from the tribunal of Pilate to the hill of Calvary.

First Station: Jesus is condemned to death.

V. We adore Thee, O Christ, and we bless Thee,
R. Because by Thy holy Cross, Thou hast redeemed the world.

Jesus, when condemned, is silent. How do I act when censured?

Pray the Our Father, the Hail Mary, and the Glory Be.

Second Station: Jesus bears His Cross.

V. We adore Thee, O Christ, and we bless Thee,
R. Because by Thy holy Cross, Thou hast redeemed the world.

Do I bear my crosses in union with the Cross of Christ?

Pray the Our Father, the Hail Mary, and the Glory Be.

Third Station: Jesus falls the first time.

V. We adore Thee, O Christ, and we bless Thee,
R. Because by Thy holy Cross, Thou hast redeemed the world.

It is the weight of my sins that caused Jesus to fall.

Pray the Our Father, the Hail Mary, and the Glory Be.

Fourth Station: Jesus meets His afflicted Mother.

V. We adore Thee, O Christ, and we bless Thee,
R. Because by Thy holy Cross, Thou hast redeemed the world.

Is my devotion to the Mother of Christ all it should be?

Pray the Our Father, the Hail Mary, and the Glory Be.

Fifth Station: The Cyrenian helps Jesus carry His Cross.

V. We adore Thee, O Christ, and we bless Thee,
R. Because by Thy holy Cross, Thou hast redeemed the world.

Unlike Simon, I am unwilling to bear the Cross with Jesus.

Pray the Our Father, the Hail Mary, and the Glory Be.

Sixth Station: Veronica wipes the face of Jesus.

V. We adore Thee, O Christ, and we bless Thee,
R. Because by Thy holy Cross, Thou hast redeemed the world.

By assisting the poor, I can help and console Jesus in His suffering.

Pray the Our Father, the Hail Mary, and the Glory Be.

Seventh Station: Jesus falls the second time.

V. We adore Thee, O Christ, and we bless Thee,
R. Because by Thy holy Cross, Thou hast redeemed the world.

It is my repeated sins that caused Jesus to fall again.

Pray the Our Father, the Hail Mary, and the Glory Be.

Eighth Station: Jesus speaks to the daughters of Jerusalem.

V. We adore Thee, O Christ, and we bless Thee,
R. Because by Thy holy Cross, Thou hast redeemed the world.

May Jesus give me the grace to weep for my sins.

Pray the Our Father, the Hail Mary, and the Glory Be.

Ninth Station: Jesus falls the third time.

V. We adore Thee, O Christ, and we bless Thee,
R. Because by Thy holy Cross, Thou hast redeemed the world.

Give me the grace, O Lord, to correct my evil habits, which cause my many falls into sin.

Pray the Our Father, the Hail Mary, and the Glory Be.

Tenth Station: Jesus is stripped of His garments.

V. We adore Thee, O Christ, and we bless Thee,
R. Because by Thy holy Cross, Thou hast redeemed the world.

Strip me, O Lord, of attachment to the things of earth.

Pray the Our Father, the Hail Mary, and the Glory Be.

Eleventh Station: Jesus is nailed to the Cross.

V. We adore Thee, O Christ, and we bless Thee,
R. Because by Thy holy Cross, Thou hast redeemed the world.

May my heart be nailed to the Cross of Jesus so as never to be separated from His love.

Pray the Our Father, the Hail Mary, and the Glory Be.

Twelfth Station: Jesus dies on the Cross.

V. We adore Thee, O Christ, and we bless Thee,
R. Because by Thy holy Cross, Thou hast redeemed the world.

Do I try to live for Jesus? He died for me.
Pray the Our Father, the Hail Mary, and the Glory Be.

Thirteenth Station: Jesus is taken down from the Cross.

V. We adore Thee, O Christ, and we bless Thee,
R. Because by Thy holy Cross, Thou hast redeemed the world.

May the Mother of Christ intercede for us in the hour of death.

Pray the Our Father, the Hail Mary, and the Glory Be.

Fourteenth Station: Jesus is placed in the sepulchre.

V. We adore Thee, O Christ, and we bless Thee,
R. Because by Thy holy Cross, Thou hast redeemed the world.

May I die to the world and to myself so that I may rise gloriously with Christ.

Pray the Our Father, the Hail Mary, and the Glory Be.

Stations of the Cross with
Marian Reflections for Reparation

(Each station begins with "We adore You, O Christ, and we bless You..." and concludes with a Marian reparation prayer.)

1. Jesus is Condemned to Death
V. We adore Thee, O Christ, and we bless Thee,
R. Because by Thy holy Cross, Thou hast redeemed the world.

Mary, you stood silent as Pilate unjustly condemned your Son. Your heart grieved, yet you surrendered to the Father's will.

Reparation: For sins of injustice, false judgment, and the condemnation of the innocent, especially in attacks against the Church and her ministers.

2. Jesus Takes Up His Cross
V. We adore Thee, O Christ, and we bless Thee,
R. Because by Thy holy Cross, Thou hast redeemed the world.

Mary, you saw the Cross laid upon His shoulders — the burden of our sins. You accepted your own share of that Cross in union with Him.

Reparation: For all who reject the crosses in their lives and for those who flee from sacrificial love.

3. Jesus Falls the First Time

V. We adore Thee, O Christ, and we bless Thee,
R. Because by Thy holy Cross, Thou hast redeemed the world.

Mary, your heart trembled as He fell beneath the weight, but your faith never faltered. You trusted the Father would strengthen Him to rise again.

Reparation: For those weighed down by sin who do not seek the mercy of God, and for those who despair after falling.

4. Jesus Meets His Blessed Mother

V. We adore Thee, O Christ, and we bless Thee,
R. Because by Thy holy Cross, Thou hast redeemed the world.

Mary, in that brief gaze, you gave Him courage. Though your souls were pierced with sorrow, your union in love was unshakable.

Reparation: For those who resist your maternal embrace and for all who refuse your guidance to your Son.

5. Simon of Cyrene Helps Jesus Carry the Cross
V. We adore Thee, O Christ, and we bless Thee,
R. Because by Thy holy Cross, Thou hast redeemed the world.

Mary, you saw a stranger drawn into the mystery of redemption. You prayed he would embrace that grace.

Reparation: For indifference to the sufferings of others and for failure to assist the weak and the poor.

6. Veronica Wipes the Face of Jesus
V. We adore Thee, O Christ, and we bless Thee,
R. Because by Thy holy Cross, Thou hast redeemed the world.

Mary, you blessed the compassion of Veronica, who dared to comfort your Son.

Reparation: For neglect of acts of mercy, and for all who refuse to see the suffering Face of Christ in their neighbor.

7. Jesus Falls the Second Time
V. We adore Thee, O Christ, and we bless Thee,
R. Because by Thy holy Cross, Thou hast redeemed the world.

Mary, you ached as He fell again, yet you prayed for His perseverance until the end.

Reparation: For those who relapse into sin and for those who encourage others to sin.

8. Jesus Meets the Women of Jerusalem
V. We adore Thee, O Christ, and we bless Thee,
R. Because by Thy holy Cross, Thou hast redeemed the world.

Mary, you heard His call for repentance and His warning of coming trials.

Reparation: For hearts that resist conversion and for the sin of ignoring the signs of God's mercy.

9. Jesus Falls the Third Time
V. We adore Thee, O Christ, and we bless Thee,
R. Because by Thy holy Cross, Thou hast redeemed the world.

Mary, your soul was pierced as He collapsed in exhaustion, yet you knew His love would not fail.

Reparation: For the sin of final impenitence and for those who harden their hearts to the last.

10. Jesus is Stripped of His Garments

V. We adore Thee, O Christ, and we bless Thee,
R. Because by Thy holy Cross, Thou hast redeemed the world.

Mary, you turned your eyes away as they stripped Him, wounding His dignity.

Reparation: For sins of impurity, immodesty, and the exploitation of the human person.

11. Jesus is Nailed to the Cross

V. We adore Thee, O Christ, and we bless Thee,
R. Because by Thy holy Cross, Thou hast redeemed the world.

Mary, you listened to the hammer's blows, each one striking your heart.

Reparation: For the violence and cruelty in the world, and for all who crucify your Son anew through grave sin.

12. Jesus Dies on the Cross

V. We adore Thee, O Christ, and we bless Thee,
R. Because by Thy holy Cross, Thou hast redeemed the world.

Mary, you stood beneath the Cross, offering your Son to the Father for our salvation.

Reparation: For rejection of His sacrifice, and for all who die without the sacraments.

13. Jesus is Taken Down from the Cross
V. We adore Thee, O Christ, and we bless Thee,
R. Because by Thy holy Cross, Thou hast redeemed the world.

Mary, you held His lifeless body, caressing the wounds of Love Himself.

Reparation: For the desecration of His Body in the Eucharist and for those who treat Holy Communion without reverence.

14. Jesus is Laid in the Tomb
V. We adore Thee, O Christ, and we bless Thee,
R. Because by Thy holy Cross, Thou hast redeemed the world.

Mary, you placed Him in the tomb with faith that the dawn of resurrection would come.

Reparation: For those who live without hope in eternal life and for all who fear death without trusting in God's mercy.

Appendix V:
Marian Promises & Indulgences

The Fifteen Promises of the Rosary

(According to tradition, given by the Blessed Virgin Mary to St. Dominic and Blessed Alan de la Roche)

1. Whoever shall faithfully serve Me by the recitation of the Rosary shall receive signal graces.

2. I promise My special protection and the greatest graces to all those who shall recite the Rosary.

3. The Rosary shall be a powerful armor against hell; it will destroy vice, decrease sin, and defeat heresies.

4. It will cause virtue and good works to flourish; it will obtain for souls the abundant mercy of God; it will withdraw the hearts of men from the love of the world and its vanities and will lift them to the desire of eternal things. Oh, that souls would sanctify themselves by this means!

5. The soul which recommends itself to Me by the recitation of the Rosary shall not perish.

6. Whoever shall recite the Rosary devoutly, applying himself to the consideration of its Sacred Mysteries, shall never be conquered by misfortune. God will not chastise him in His justice; he shall not perish by an unprovided death; if he be just, he shall remain in the grace of God and become worthy of eternal life.

7. Whoever shall have a true devotion for the Rosary shall not die without the Sacraments of the Church.

8. Those who are faithful to recite the Rosary shall have during their life and at their death the light of God and the plenitude of His graces; at the moment of death, they shall participate in the merits of the Saints in Paradise.

9. I shall deliver from purgatory those who have been devoted to the Rosary.

10. The faithful children of the Rosary shall merit a high degree of glory in Heaven.

11. You shall obtain all you ask of Me by the recitation of the Rosary.

12. All those who propagate the Holy Rosary shall be aided by Me in their necessities.

13. I have obtained from My Divine Son that all the advocates of the Rosary shall have for intercessors the entire celestial court during their life and at the hour of death.

14. All who recite the Rosary are My sons, and brothers of My only Son Jesus Christ.

15. Devotion to My Rosary is a great sign of predestination.

Indulgences Attached to Marian Devotions

The Catholic Church, in her maternal solicitude, attaches indulgences to many Marian devotions to encourage the faithful to draw closer to Jesus through Mary.

Below is a summary of notable indulgences related to the Rosary and other Marian prayers, according to current norms and traditional practice.

RECITATION OF THE MOST HOLY ROSARY

Plenary Indulgence when the Rosary is recited:

1. In a church, oratory, religious community, or family group.
2. Or in a pious association of the faithful.
3. Or when several of the faithful gather for any good purpose and pray together.

Conditions for plenary indulgence:

1. Sacramental Confession (within about 20 days before or after).
2. Eucharistic Communion.
3. Prayer for the intentions of the Holy Father (e.g., one Our Father and one Hail Mary).
4. Complete detachment from all sin, even venial.

Partial Indulgence for devout recitation outside the above conditions.

Note: In public recitation, the mysteries must be announced and meditated upon; in private recitation, announcing them suffices.

ANGELUS OR REGINA CAELI DURING EASTER

Partial Indulgence each time it is devoutly recited.

Plenary Indulgence once a month for those who recite it daily and fulfill the usual conditions.

LITANY OF LORETO

Partial Indulgence for devout recitation.

MEMORARE

Partial Indulgence for devout recitation.

SALVE REGINA & SUB TUUM PRAESIDIUM

Partial Indulgence each time they are recited with devotion.

WEARING THE SCAPULAR OF OUR LADY OF MOUNT CARMEL

1. Partial Indulgence for devout kissing of the scapular.
2. Other indulgences apply under specific Confraternity or Third Order rules.

ACT OF CONSECRATION TO THE IMMACULATE HEART OF MARY

Partial Indulgence for any approved formula recited devoutly.

PARTICIPATION IN A MARIAN PILGRIMAGE OR FEAST

1. Plenary Indulgence for participating devoutly in a solemn Marian procession.
2. Partial Indulgence for devout participation in any local Marian devotion.

Important Reminder:

All indulgences are applicable to the souls in purgatory.

To gain a plenary indulgence, the faithful must also be free from all attachment to sin, even venial. If this is lacking, the indulgence will be partial.

Appendix VI:
Additional Reflections

Reflections from Fulton Sheen on Mary

Ave Maria

"Mary is not a goddess, but she is the Mother of God. This is the most exalted title that can be given to any creature, for it means that she bore in her womb the Eternal Word made flesh. If we deny her this honor, we diminish the reality of the Incarnation. She is the bridge between Heaven and earth, the new Eve whose obedience reversed the disobedience of the first."

— Fulton J. Sheen, *The World's First Love*

Fiat Voluntas Tua

"Mary's 'Fiat' was not a single word spoken in Nazareth; it was the song of her whole life. She lived in the shadow of the Cross even as she cradled the Infant in Bethlehem. Her surrender to God was total — from the manger to Calvary, she never withdrew her 'Yes.' And because of her, God found a dwelling place among men."

— Fulton J. Sheen, *The World's First Love*

Mater Dolorosa

"At the foot of the Cross, Mary was not a rebel against the will of God; she was the new Eve standing beside the new Adam. She did not cry out against the nails that pierced her Son, for her own heart was pierced as well. In the supreme act of faith, she offered her Son back to the Father who had given Him."

— Fulton J. Sheen, *The World's First Love*

Virgo Fidelis

"Mary's faith never wavered, not at Nazareth, not at Bethlehem, and not at Calvary. She is the model of the faithful soul who clings to God's promises even when the sword of sorrow seems to cut them to pieces. In her constancy, we see the perfect image of the Church herself, which never abandons her Lord."

— Fulton J. Sheen, *The World's First Love*

Regina Caeli

"Mary was crowned Queen not because she was the Mother of Jesus only, but because she cooperated in His redemptive mission. A queen shares in the dignity and work of the king, and so Mary shares in the glory of her Son. In Heaven she reigns, not to keep her subjects distant, but to draw them ever closer to Christ."

— Fulton J. Sheen, *The World's First Love*

Mater Misericordiae

"Mary's mercy is the reflection of God's mercy. She sees in every sinner the soul her Son died to save, and so she extends her motherly care to the ends of the earth. We go to her not because she replaces Christ, but because she leads us unfailingly to Him."

— Fulton J. Sheen, *The World's First Love*

Stella Maris

"As the sailor looks to the star to find his way to port, so the Christian looks to Mary to find the way to Christ. She does not shine with her own light, but with the reflected light of her Son. Her whole mission is to point beyond herself to the safe harbor of salvation."

— Fulton J. Sheen, *The World's First Love*

Tota Pulchra Es

"Mary is the one creature who was never the slave of sin. In her Immaculate Conception, we see the masterpiece of God's creative love. If we could make our own mother perfect, how much more would God make His? In her, beauty and holiness are perfectly one."

— Fulton J. Sheen, *The World's First Love*

Mater Ecclesiae

"At Pentecost, Mary was in the upper room, praying with the Apostles. The Mother of Jesus became the Mother of the Church, just as she had become the Mother of John at Calvary. Her maternity extends to all the members of Christ's Mystical Body, for she is forever united to Him."

— Fulton J. Sheen, *The World's First Love*

Advocata Nostra

"Mary is not a lawyer pleading before a reluctant judge; she is the Mother standing before her Son. She knows that to ask Him for mercy on our behalf is to ask for something He has already died to give. Her advocacy is not to change His heart, but to open ours to receive the graces He longs to pour out."

— Fulton J. Sheen, *The World's First Love*

Spes Nostra

"In the darkness of our trials, Mary stands as a sign of hope. She has walked the road of faith, suffered the sword of sorrow, and seen the victory of the Resurrection. She reminds us that the last word in the Christian story is not the Cross, but the empty tomb."

— Fulton J. Sheen, *The World's First Love*

Immaculata

"Mary is the world's solitary boast. In her, we see what humanity was meant to be: pure, holy, and full of grace. Her life tells us that sanctity is possible, and that God can take what is lowly and raise it to heights beyond our imagining."

— Fulton J. Sheen, *The World's First Love*

Reflections from the Saints on Mary

Ave Maria

"Never be afraid of loving the Blessed Virgin too much. You can never love her more than Jesus did.

— **St. Maximilian Kolbe**

Fiat Mihi

"In dangers, in doubts, in difficulties, think of Mary, call upon Mary. Let her name be ever on your lips, ever in your heart, and that you may obtain the help of her prayers, never depart from the example of her holy life."

— **St. Bernard of Clairvaux** (*De Maria Numquam Satis*)

Mater Dolorosa

"Truly, O Blessed Mother, a sword has pierced your heart. For only by passing through your heart could the sword enter the flesh of your Son. Indeed, after your Jesus — who belongs to everyone, but especially to you — gave up His life, the cruel spear opened His side and would not touch His soul. But it did pierce yours. His soul was no longer there, but yours could not be torn away."

— **St. Bernard of Clairvaux**

Virgo Fidelis

"Do not be afraid to receive Mary into your home, into your heart. She is the faithful Virgin who never abandons those entrusted to her. She will lead you unfailingly to Christ, for that is her only desire."

— **St. John Paul II** (*Redemptoris Mater*)

Regina Caeli

"Mary has been given to us as a model of holiness. In contemplating her, we see how to live for God and neighbor; in praying to her, we are drawn into communion with her Son; in imitating her, we become more like Christ."

— **Pope Benedict XVI**

Mater Misericordiae

"As the moon is between the sun and the earth, so is Mary placed between God and us. She receives the light of grace from the Sun of Justice and passes it on to us, poor dwellers of this earth, darkened by sin."

— **St. Louis de Montfort** (*True Devotion to Mary*)

Stella Maris

"If the winds of temptation arise, if you are driven upon the rocks of tribulation, look to the star, call upon Mary. If you are tossed upon the waves of pride, ambition, envy, or rivalry, look to the star, call upon Mary. If anger or avarice or the allurements of the flesh dash against the ship of your soul, look to Mary."

— St. Bernard of Clairvaux

Tota Pulchra Es

"You are all fair, O Mary, and the original stain is not in you. You are the glory of Jerusalem, you are the joy of Israel, you are the honor of our people."

— Antiphon from the Liturgy of the Hours

Mater Ecclesia

"From the Cross, the Lord entrusted all humanity to Mary in the person of John. And from that hour, Mary's motherhood took on a universal dimension, for she cares for every disciple of Christ in every generation."

— St. John Paul II

Advocata Nostra

"As Jesus is the one Mediator between God and men, so Mary is the mediatrix between Jesus and us. Not that she adds to His work, but that she helps us to receive it, making our prayers more acceptable and our hearts more ready to obey."

— St. Alphonsus Liguori (*Glories of Mary*)

Spes Nostra

"Mary is the surest, easiest, shortest, and most perfect way of approaching Jesus and will surrender herself to the souls who wish to approach Him through her."

— St. Louis de Montfort

Immaculata

"O Mary, conceived without sin, pray for us who have recourse to thee."

— Invocation revealed to St. Catherine Labouré, *1830*

WHEN CALVARY BECOMES THE NURSERY

Have you ever wondered what it means to be a child of God? The Catechism of the Catholic Church teaches us that through baptism, we become "an adopted child of God, who has become a partaker of the divine nature, member of Christ and co-heir with him, and a temple of the Holy Spirit." (CCCC 1265)

Similarly, the Church teaches us that when Our Blessed Lord spoke these words from the Cross: "Woman, behold your son, Son behold your Mother" (Jn. 19:26), we were given at that moment, the title, 'Children of Mary.'

To help flesh out this teaching on spiritual adoption in a deeper way, we will once again ponder some of the words shared by Archbishop Sheen earlier in this book.

"An angel of light went out and came to where a humble virgin of Nazareth knelt in prayer, and said, "Hail, full of grace!" These were not words; they were the Word. "And the Word became flesh." This was the first Annunciation.

Nine months passed, and once more an angel from that great white Throne of Light came down to shepherds on Judean hills, teaching them the joy of a "Gloria in Excelsis," and bidding them worship Him Whom the world could not contain, a "Babe wrapped in swaddling clothes and laid in a manger." Eternity became time, Divinity incarnate, God a man; Omnipotence was discovered in bonds. In the language of Saint Luke, Mary "brought forth her firstborn Son... and laid Him in a manger." This was the first Nativity.

Then came Nazareth and the carpenter shop where one can imagine the Divine Boy, straitened until baptized with a baptism of blood, fashioning a little cross in anticipation of a great Cross that would one day be His on Calvary. One can also imagine Him in the evening of a day of labour at the bench, stretching out His arms in exhausted relaxation, while the setting sun traced on the opposite wall the shadow of a man on a cross. One can, too, imagine His Mother seeing in each nail the prophecy and the telltale of a day when men would carpenter to a Cross the One who carpentered the universe.

Nazareth passed into Calvary, and the nails of the shop into the nails of human malignity. From the Cross, He completed His last will and testament. He had already committed His blood to the Church, His garments to His enemies, a thief to Paradise, and would soon commend His body to the grave and His soul to His Heavenly Father. To whom, then, could He give the two treasures which He loved above all others, Mary and John? He would bequeath them to one another, giving at once a son to His Mother and a Mother to His friend. "Woman!" It was the second Annunciation! The midnight hour, the silent room, the ecstatic prayer had given way to the mount of Calvary, the darkened sky, and a Son hanging on a Cross. Yet, what consolation! It was only an angel who made the first Annunciation, but it is God's own sweet voice which makes the second.

"Behold your son!" It was the second Nativity! Mary had brought forth her First-born without labor, in the cave of Bethlehem; she now brings forth her second-born, John, in the labors of the Cross. At this moment, Mary is undergoing the pains of childbirth, not only for her second-born, who is John, but also for the millions who will be born to her in Christian ages as 'Children of Mary'. Now we can understand why Christ was called 'her Firstborn'. It was not because she was to have other children by the blood of flesh, but because she was to have other children by the blood of her heart. Truly, indeed, the Divine condemnation against Eve is now renewed against the new Eve, Mary, for she is bringing forth her children in sorrow.

Mary, then, is not only the Mother of Our Lord and Saviour, Jesus Christ, but she is also our Mother, and this not by a title of courtesy, not by legal fiction, not by a mere figure of speech, but by the right of bringing us forth in sorrow at the foot of the Cross. It was by weakness and disobedience at the foot of the tree of Good and Evil that Eve lost the title, Mother of the Living; it is at the foot of the tree of the Cross that Mary, by sacrifice and obedience, regained for us the title, Mother of the Living. What a destiny to have the Mother of God as my Mother and Jesus as my Brother!

Oh, the joy that can come in accepting this profound reality that Mary is our Mother and Jesus is our Brother. What a tremendous gift we have received from God the Father! But what does this gift entail? Our Blessed Lord gave us His Mother from His Cross on Calvary, but what are our responsibilities to her? And what are her responsibilities to us?

The Catholic Church teaches that when we die, we will be judged by Christ and will have to make an accounting of lives. Some of us may wonder what questions God will ask of us. Did I feed the poor? Did I avoid sin? Did I make peace instead of war? But what if I told you that one of the questions Jesus might ask us would be:

"Did You Love My Mother?"

Now, for me, pondering this question has caused me many a restless night. To be honest, I had ignored Mary for many years. I had given her lip service, with a few half-hearted rosaries and novenas. I had been guilty of saying that Mary was my Mother — but in name only. In actual fact, I was not allowing Mary to be my Mother. With time, I started to think, did not Christ desire to share with me His Kingdom and all its treasures? Why would I choose to ignore the one person that God chose to be His Mother and mine? Why would I choose to reject the love, guidance, graces, and blessings that the Blessed

Mother wanted to give me, as she certainly gave Our Lord during His life?

Well, after searching my heart and taking stock of what I had done and what I had failed to do with regard to the Blessed Mother, I truly started to experience a sense of sorrow. I knew that I needed somehow to apologize in some way to the Blessed Virgin Mary. But sadly, this apology would take a while to materialize because, as you might know, sometimes the three hardest words to say in life are: "I am sorry!" Fortunately for me, by God's grace and Our Lady's intercession, I eventually apologized to the Blessed Mother. But that apology came after a real-life situation, which provided me with a kind of 'epiphany.'

A Reckless One

We all know stories of drunk drivers who get behind the wheel of a car and kill innocent people. Sadly, this story is repeated time and time again. There are casualties on both sides of these tragic stories: the families devastated by their loss and the drivers who have to live with the consequences of their bad decisions.

With this thought, I started to ask myself, how would I respond if a drunk driver asked me for mercy after killing my child? For some strange coincidence, while I was pondering on this thought, I saw out of the corner of my eye a crucifix hanging on the wall in my living room. As I looked upon it for a few moments, my epiphany came to me. At that moment, I saw the connection between the drunk driver killing an innocent victim with his car and the stark reality that it was my sins that caused the death of an innocent victim, Jesus Christ, who had to pay for my sins by dying on the Cross.

I had realized that it was my sin that nailed Jesus to His Cross. I was guilty of His death. I was the reckless one who now needed to apologize to the Victim's Mother for the role that I played in the death of her Son. That victim was Jesus, and the Mother of the victim was the Blessed Virgin Mary.

But how does one apologize to the Blessed Mother? Let me share a few words from Archbishop Sheen that will help.

He writes, "If you can stand the gaze of a Crucifix long enough, you will discover these truths. First, if sin cost Him Who is Innocence, so much, then I who am guilty cannot take it lightly; second, in all the world, there is only one thing worse than sin, and that is to forget I am a sinner; third, more bitter than the Crucifixion must be my rejection of that Love by which I was redeemed."

"There is no escaping the one thing necessary in the Christian life, namely, saving our souls and purchasing the glorious liberty of the children of God.

The crucifixion ends, but Christ endures. Sorrows pass, but we remain. Therefore, we must never come down from the supreme end and purpose of life, the salvation of our souls."

"What had she done to deserve the Seven Swords? What crimes had she committed to robbing her of her Son? She had done nothing, but we have. We have sinned against her Divine Son, we have sentenced him to the Cross, and in sinning against him, we wounded her.

In fact, we thrust into her hands the greatest of all griefs, for she was not losing a brother, or a sister, or a father, or a mother, or even just a son -- she was losing God. And what greater sorrow is there than this!

Finally, we should mourn for the greatest of all reasons, namely, because of what our sins have done to him. If we had been less proud, his crown of thorns would have been less piercing; if we had been less avaricious, the nails in the hands would have been less burning; if we had traveled less in the devious ways of sin, his feet would not have been so deeply dug with steel; if our speech had been less biting, his lips would have been less parched; if we had been less sinful, his agony would have been shorter; if we had loved more, he would have been hated less."

It may be difficult, but may I encourage you to take a moment to reflect on your relationship with the Blessed Mother and to see if an apology might be in order? Just imagine yourself approaching her at the foot of the cross with St. Mary Magdalene weeping on her knees beside her and St. John standing there with you. Look up to our Crucified Lord and then take a few moments to reflect on His death. Then, may I encourage you to reach out as I did and apologize to the Blessed Mother for the role you played in the death of her Son.

I recall a song written in 2001 by Fr. Eugene O'Reilly, CSsR. The song was entitled 'Father I Have Sinned' (The Prodigal Son). The lyrics are beautiful and provide great consolation to many 'prodigals' like myself.

Having made my confession and asking for pardon, I envisioned the Blessed Mother singing the words of the chorus in that beautiful song: I forgive you. I love you. You are mine. Take my hand. Go in peace, sin no more, beloved one.

For myself, I knew at once that when I made my apology to the Blessed Mother, my life changed; my relationship with her was strengthened. I rejoiced in thinking how great her joy would be to shelter under her mantle, one more of her Son's lost sheep!

Our Mother, Our Champion

I will leave you this one last pearl of wisdom from Archbishop Sheen:

"May I recommend that if you have never before prayed to Mary, do so now. Can you not see that if Christ himself willed to be physically formed in her for nine months and then be spiritually formed by her for thirty years? It is to her that we must go to learn how to have Christ formed in us? Only she who raised Christ can raise a Christian.

"There are many falsehoods told about the Catholic Church: One of them is that Catholics adore Mary. This is absolutely untrue. Mary is a creature, human, not divine. Catholics do not adore Mary. That would be idolatry. But they do reverence her.

And to those Christians who have forgotten Mary, may we ask if it is proper for them to forget her whom He remembered on the Cross? Will they bear no love for that woman through the portals of whose flesh, as the Gate of Heaven, He came to earth?

One of the reasons why so many Christians have lost a belief in the Divinity of Christ is because they lost all affection for her upon whose white body, as a Tower of Ivory, that Infant climbed "to kiss upon her lips a mystic rose."

There is not a Christian in the entire world who reverences Mary, who does not acknowledge Jesus her Son to be in Truth, the Son of the Living God. The prudent Christ on the Cross knew the prudent way to preserve belief in His Divinity, for whom better than a Mother knows her son?"

"And now at the end of his life, the Roman governor could say: "Your own nation...has delivered you up to me." Thus did he who is King of Kings become socially poor and an outcast from the snobs of the earth, so that through that abandonment we might become -- let us pause at the very thought of it -- children of God!"

"There is no stopping it except by reversing the process by which we drove God out of the world, namely by relighting the lamp of faith in the souls of men."

"His soul that was burning and His Heart that was on fire. He was thirsting for the souls of men. The Shepherd was lonely without His sheep; the Creator was yearning for His creatures; the First-born was looking for His brethren."

Christ is waiting for our response. Our Brother Christ, who is also our Lord and our God, waits at the side of our crib, in the nursery called Calvary. He presents to us His Mother as our loving helper. He keeps His promise, "I shall not leave you orphaned".

Christ said, "My sheep hear my voice. I know them, and they follow me." The Good Lord knows each one of us, and he knows His Mother. Think of how much easier it will be for those souls who, like the Apostle John, 'took Mary into their home'. The calming effect of a Mother; the blessing; the encouragement; the companionship and the fellowship that John experienced by being obedient to Christ's words, "Behold your Mother", these are the graces that await us, her children.

When we read the scriptures, we see that the Virgin Mary and Christ are inseparable. Wherever Our

185

Lord is mentioned, she is found there near Him. When Christ comes again in glory and searches for his sheep, would it not be easier for Him to find us if His Mother has taken up residence with us and she is by our side? What a great advocate and companion we will have on that day when we are reunited with our Brother and Lord.

Let us not be afraid to take Mary into our home, and to accept the adoption that God has arranged for us at the foot of Calvary.

Calvary has truly become a nursery, and each one of us has been given three special gifts at the foot of the Cross. The first is the Blessed Virgin Mary, who has become our Mother. The second is our own crib. And the third is our own cross.

Please know that there are many cribs in this nursery alongside yours. Our Blessed Mother Mary is there to care for us and to lead us to our Saviour, for we do not save our souls alone, but only in companionship with others.

Each of us, too, has a cross. Our Lord said: "If any man will follow me" (Mark 8:34). He did not say: "Take up my cross." My cross is not the same as yours, and yours is not the same as mine. Every cross in the world is tailor-made, custom-built, patterned to fit one and no one else.

That is why we say: "My cross is hard." We assume that other people's crosses are lighter, forgetful that the only reason our cross is hard is simply that it is our own. Our Lord did not make His Cross; it was made for Him. So, yours is made by the circumstances of your life, and by your routine duties. That is why it fits so tightly. Crosses are not made by machines but by God.

I pray that this journey of discovery given by Archbishop Fulton J. Sheen has touched your heart. Each of us has a cross to carry and a crib to rest in.

Hopefully, there will be times in our lives when we will look up from our cribs and thank the Good Lord for all that He has done for us and the many opportunities he has given to us to love Him and Our Blessed Mother.

Remember that the cribs of God's children are located at the foot of the Cross. May we be so blessed to look upon the cross each day from our cribs and remember the love that Jesus Christ has for us in that he laid down his life for us on the Cross.

Let us not be afraid to fully embrace the spiritual adoption that God has arranged for us at the foot of Calvary, to become 'Children of Mary.'

And may those sweet words of our Blessed Lord, "Behold Thy Mother," be that gentle reminder that you are not alone and that you belong to the family of God.

Permit me to close with a short, childlike prayer I often say through the day:

"Jesus, Mary, and Joseph, I Love You! Never leave me! Please save souls, including my own! Amen."

Concluding Word
Sent from the Foot of the Cross

From Calvary resounds the command of Christ: "Behold your mother." This is no suggestion, but a gift and a mission. To behold Mary is to welcome her into the intimacy of our homes, our prayer, our very hearts. She is Mother of the Church, Mother of priests, Mother of souls longing for holiness. Fulton Sheen reminds us that whenever we draw close to Mary, she points us unerringly to her Son.

As these reflections end, let them begin anew in your life. Entrust your crosses to Mary's hands; consecrate your joys to her Immaculate Heart. With her, the darkest nights become dawn, and every suffering can be united to the redeeming love of Jesus. May our last word echo the first command: *Behold your Mother.*

About the Author

Allan Smith is a Catholic evangelist, radio host, and spiritual director who has spent over a decade proclaiming the wisdom of Archbishop Fulton J. Sheen to audiences around the world. As the founder of Bishop Sheen Today, he has edited and published dozens of classic Sheen titles, including 'The Cries of Jesus from the Cross' and 'Lord, Teach Us to Pray'.

A passionate promoter of Eucharistic Reparation and devotion to the Holy Face of Jesus, Allan regularly speaks at parish missions, leads retreats, and hosts weekly radio broadcasts across Canada, the United States, Ireland, Australia and the Philippines. His work has helped reintroduce Sheen's powerful spiritual legacy to a new generation.

He lives in Canada with his family and continues his mission of calling souls to deeper intimacy with Christ through the example of saints like St. Thérèse of Lisieux and the timeless teachings of Fulton Sheen.

To learn more or to access free devotional resources, visit our two websites at:

www.bishopsheentoday.com

www.holyfacemiracle.com

A Personal Invitation

Over the years, I have had the privilege of helping souls draw closer to Christ through prayer, silence, and the beautiful wisdom of Archbishop Fulton J. Sheen.

If this devotional has nourished your heart, you may also find these works helpful in your journey of faith:

Advent and Christmas with

Archbishop Fulton J. Sheen

- A Devotional Journey of Waiting, Welcoming, and Living the Mystery

Daily readings and gentle reflections to guide the heart from hope to joy — from the quiet longing of Advent to the radiant wonder of Christmas.

Priest, Prophet & King

- Meditations on Identity, Mission, and the Call to Holiness

Reflections on what it means to truly belong to Christ — in our families, vocations, and daily life.

The Sheen Mission Series

Collected Meditations

- Over 100 of the Richest Reflections from Retreats, Radio, and Prayer

A treasury to keep on the nightstand — for those ten-minute moments of quiet that become encounters with God.

May every book you read be an open door to the heart of Christ.

May these works draw you deeper into prayer, trust, peace, and surrender.

And may the Child of Bethlehem be born again in you.

Come, Lord Jesus.

To learn more or to stay connected:
www.bishopsheentoday.com

About the Sheen Mission Series

The Sheen Mission Series is a four-volume spiritual journey inspired by Archbishop Fulton J. Sheen. Each book is designed as a devotional companion — guiding the faithful in prayer, reparation, and renewal through the Holy Face of Jesus, the Cross, the Eucharist and the maternal love of Our Blessed Mother.

The series can be read in any order, yet together it forms a complete mission of grace:

- **Volume I – *The Holy Face and the Little Way***
  Walk with St. Thérèse of Lisieux in her Little Way of love, united to the devotion of the Holy Face of Jesus.

- **Volume II – *Behold Your Mother***
  Enter into Mary's tender care at the foot of the Cross and discover the strength of her Seven Sorrows.

- **Volume III – *The Cross and the Last Words***
  Pray with Archbishop Sheen at Calvary as he opens the treasures of the Seven Last Words of Christ.

- **Volume IV – *Lord, Show Us Thy Face and We Shall Be Saved***

A mission of light and transformation, centered on the Eucharist and the saving power of Christ's Face.

The Sheen Mission Series invites you to walk with Archbishop Fulton J. Sheen in prayer, reparation, and renewal — a journey of the Holy Face, the Cross, the Eucharist, and Our Blessed Mother.

J M J